THE TWO LIVES OF BABY DOE

The Two Lives of
BABY DOE

by GORDON LANGLEY HALL

illustrated with photographs

MACRAE SMITH COMPANY:
PHILADELPHIA

The author acknowledges with many thanks the permission to quote the poem "Epitaph" by the late Gerald Gould, kindly given to him by the poet's literary executor, Mr. Michael Ayrton.

For
DURANT L. MACRAE

AUTHOR'S NOTE

My very real thanks go to the people of Denver and Leadville, Colorado, who so generously helped me with my research undertaken at a time when back in New York the woman I loved lay desperately ill. Colorado historians, librarians, authors, booksellers, socialites, housewives and newspapermen could not have been more friendly to the rather young interloper from across the water who was invading their territory to write his own interpretation of their most fabulous heroine. To me the fabled hospitality of the West was realistically proven.

I would like to thank especially Mrs. Roy B. Adams (Brownie Adams), archaeologist and explorer, who arranged for me to meet a number of prominent Denver citizens at her beautiful Vagabond House; Mrs. Agnes Wright Spring, State Historian, The State Historical Society of Colorado, who, on a very warm summer's day, wheeled in the vast Baby Doe archives upon a large trolley; Mrs. Delores Renze, Colorado State Archivist; Mrs. Laura A. Ekstrom, Assistant Librarian, Colorado State Museum; Mrs. Alys Freeze, Head of the Western History Department, the Public Library, the City and County of Denver, whose documentation of facts is a credit to Denver, and her staff, especially Jim Davis and Christine Larsen; Miss Caroline Bancroft, author, historian and Tabor authority who generously and readily put her own findings at my disposal in a way that always bespeaks the true student; The Reverend Father Edward L. Horgan, formerly of the Church of the Annunciation, Leadville, Baby Doe's loyal friend;

AUTHOR'S NOTE

Mrs. H. A. Horton, President, Woman's Press Club of Denver; Mr. and Mrs. H. McElreavy; Fred A. Rosenstock; Mrs. Gano Everett (Laurena H.) Senter, Parliamentarian, and Mrs. William Fletcher (Chloë) Russell, both of whom as teen-agers retained vivid memories of the aging Baby Doe; John T. Challoner, Historian, Oshkosh Public Library, Wisconsin; The New York Historical Society; Paul W. Shipley, Chief of the Bureau of Vital Statistics and Data Processing, Sacramento, State of California; Laura P. Crane, Reference Librarian, The State Historical Society of Missouri, Columbia, Missouri; Margaret A. Whalen, Research Librarian, Maine State Library, Augusta, Maine; Elroy F. Goebel, Sr., Superintendent, Mount Olivet Cemetery Association, Denver; Mrs. Theresa O'Brien, Carol Brown, Kurt Lani, and Ruth Miller, guides at the Tabor Opera House, Leadville; Mary Jane Malavar and Emmett Connors, guides at the Matchless Mine, Leadville; Dorothy Morgan, Deputy Registrar of Vital Statistics, Pasadena, California; the University of Berkeley, Berkeley, California; Hazel F. Shanks; Mrs. Donald (Eleanor) Koontz; Jack Foster, Editor, *Rocky Mountain News*, Denver; Mrs. Ralph Peck; A. Parks McCombs, M.D.; Mrs. James H. (Belle Donnelly) Hayes; Isabel L. Whitney; Elizabeth-Anne Stuart-Hogg; Mr. and Mrs. Pierce Trowbridge Wetter; and—last but not least— my loyal typist and friend, Gertrude Young.

GORDON LANGLEY HALL

New York City,
1962

CONTENTS

EPITAPH

Life did her wrong, and death will do her wrong.
   Rest was for her too fond, and change too rough.
Not love could make her mortal, and not song
   Could give her immortality enough.

She had such beauty as, when all else goes rotten,
   Lurks in the flower beneath the darkness furled.
Here lies, lone buried in a place forgotten,
   The girl that was the wonder of the world.

GERALD GOULD

THE TWO LIVES OF BABY DOE

Chapter One

California Gulch

Nот far below timber line and over ten thousand feet above sea level, California Gulch contained the best placer diggings found up to that time in Colorado. A certain Abe Lee, together with other Southerners from Georgia recently arrived from Russell Gulch, had discovered them. Like Horace Tabor, they had met only with bad luck in Cache Creek; then, meeting some Iowans, they had followed the Arkansas River almost to its source. From there the latter explored one gulch and the Georgians another. Abe Lee persevered in panning the sandy soil until on April 27, 1860, he really

[15]

did find gold. Excitedly looking at the rewarding pay dirt he shouted, "O my God! I've got all California in this here pan." Unknowingly he had given the gulch its name. It was located off the southwest side of Ball Mountain, one of the lower elevations of the Mosquito Range.

When Horace and Augusta Tabor arrived, they found about fifty miners already encamped in the gulch but no women, so once more Augusta was the first member of her sex in camp. Quickly Hod and the boarders staked out claims in the snow, then everybody stopped work to build Augusta and Maxcy a windowless cabin with sod roof. The wagon was broken up to provide, with the addition of green logs, crude furniture: three-legged stools, provision shelves, a table and sleeping bunks. Sadly Augusta went inside for she knew that the oxen had to be killed.

> *The first thing after camping was to have the faith-ful old oxen butchered that had brought us all the way from Kansas—yes, from the Missouri River three years before. We divided the meat with the miners in the gulch, for they were without provisions or ammunition.*

Augusta had already faced hardships that would have been unbelievable for anybody but a New England woman living in that ambitious age. A flat-chested old maid of twenty-four when she married "Hod"—her last and only chance—she had readily agreed to help him seek a fortune in the West when the Kansas-Nebraska Act of 1854 had given new impetus to the North and South to find recruits for their rival "Pilgrim" settlements.

The honeymoon, from Westport (Kansas City) on, had been spent in an ox-drawn wagon, and their tenure of a deserted homestead in Kansas had been made precarious by the warring between the Slave Staters, the Free Staters and the Federal officials, with the edgy Pawnees, awaiting the outcome, making their farming and chicken raising a dubious procedure.

News of gold in the Pike's Peak region had drawn them on and Augusta, refusing to return for safety to Maine, pressed on over the almost roadless plains, shaken with fever and ague and fearful for the survival of their newborn son Maxcy. Despite the grueling routine of washing, ironing and cooking with only buffalo chips for fuel, Augusta saw beauty in the prairie chickens and antelopes and the awesome white thunderheads in the Western sky. Sometimes the wind was so bad that the wagon had to be staked to the ground, and thieving Indians following in their wake made overnight guards necessary.

Clerks, lawyers and doctors mingled with farm workers toiling footsore, hungry and often in rags across the endless prairie. Death came to many, and even cannibalism was not unknown. Augusta made Baby Maxcy's clothes—shirts, underwear and pants—of flour, salt and sugar sacks.

Settled in Denver, Augusta had found that her

baking and other domestic ventures earned them enough money to settle the cost of the farm left behind in Kansas, which Horace hoped never to see again.

At Pike's Peak, Augusta's heart had leapt at the beauty of the park, which "looked like a cultivated field with rivulets coursing through and herds of antelopes in the distance." But they suffered from extreme cold, and water was so bitter that even the cattle refused it, and although they did find quantities of fine gold in Cache Creek, it was hard to separate from the black sand with which it was liberally mixed. Augusta's hands grew red and cracked from trying to separate it through her bare fingers.

Hod cut timber to make sluice boxes, but the results were almost negative. Augusta, a capable penwoman, wrote in her journal, "For four weeks we worked there. Our supplies were almost gone, and we felt discouraged. It had been a long year since we had heard of the loved ones at home."

Once more on the move, they had maintained their slow, zigzagging progress by repeatedly crossing the river, fierce from the spring rains. Suddenly, during one such fording operation, the wagon containing Augusta and the baby had rolled from a rocky plateau right into the swirling maelstrom of a mountain current. Augusta screamed for help but—high on the ledge above—there was nothing that Hod and his companions could do. Like a matchbox the wagon bed detached itself from the wheels and twisting madly floated downstream. Seeing it fill with water, Augusta, clutching her screaming child under one arm, had the presence of mind to plunge into the river as they brushed against the shore. Desperately she clutched at some small saplings growing out of a crevice, managing, in spite of the struggling child, to hold on until help came.

Eventually the wagon and wheels were also recovered, and finally on May 8, 1860, a momentous day in the lives of Horace A.W. and Augusta Tabor, they had arrived in fabled California Gulch.

Actually their new neighbors had another purpose in building Augusta a house, being tired of doing their own cooking and laundry. Perhaps Augusta would oblige?

Augusta was only too pleased. This way, even if Hod did not find gold, they would have a little income. Ruefully she thought that she had "nothing to feed them but poor beef and dried apples." Sensibly she had brought some gold scales which proved to be the only ones in California Gulch. For a small charge she weighed the miners' gold dust and would sometimes mind small quantities for them in her blouse or beneath her large skirts. It was literally true that Augusta Tabor's bosom was the first bank in Colorado!

Her little cabin was situated in the upper end of the Gulch, and from the door she daily watched the influx of fortune hunters, followed always by the painted ladies and professional gamblers. In a few weeks, over ten thousand men had arrived in what was first called Bough City and later Oro City. Along the seven-mile stretch of gulch that ran parallel to the southern boundary of today's Leadville, log cabins, brush huts and tents sprang up overnight. Some prospectors camped like caravan dwellers in their own wagons. Augusta was appointed postmistress and also opened a small log store, a replica of which now stands in front of the Tabor Opera House, Leadville. "I was very happy that summer," she wrote in her diary.

No accurate figures exist for those days but Caroline Bancroft records in her book *Tabor's Matchless Mine and Lusty Leadville,* "It has been assumed that some $2,000,000 worth of gold was taken out that summer. Claims took up every foot of the gulch from its source down to the spot where it joined the Arkansas. Each day men were working hard with gold pans, rockers, Long Toms and sluice boxes from early dawn until the light failed. Oro City's life was one of frenzied activity."

The claims yielded varied riches. As Miss Bancroft points out, "Tabor's claim netted him $5,000 that summer while that of the man just below him on the creek bed brought in $80,000. This variance was probably due to the erratic strength of the trickle of water in the stream bed which had been depositing gold in unpredictable pockets during its centuries-long flow."

Abe Lee became the city's recorder, and murder, claim jumping and stealing were quickly settled by the short end of a rope. Among the first miners little thievery took place, but as the town grew there was always the chance of outlaws' passing through. Few wives accompanied their husbands into the wilds. While some men, affected by months of lonely mountain prospecting, actually became woman haters, most of them patronized the dance halls, sporting houses and gambling dens. Some of the painted ladies hailed from cultured homes in the East. The most colorful of these was a Boston girl named Nellie who never did reveal her surname. In Oro City they called her "Red Stockings." Twenty years old, cultivated and well-spoken, she entertained the better class of prospector, and galloped about the Gulch on a chestnut stallion, her dark hair bedecked with red ribbons—with stockings to match.

Red Stockings had brought from the East a wardrobe fit to kill. To one or two special customers she told her life story. She had earned the disfavor of her wealthy New England family by falling in love with a French officer during a European trip. Back in America under a cloud of criticism, she had run off with a gambler to spite the relatives, but found him a drunkard; and so, leaving him, she had decided to seek a quick fortune in the gold fields. Augusta was shocked that a fellow New England female should behave so outrageously, but nothing she said made the girl change her ways. By the end of the following summer Red Stockings had made her pile, and disappeared with a hundred thousand dollars to "become a fine wife and mother in Nevada."

Father Machebeuf, who had come to build a log church, fell ill with mountain fever. Augusta cared for him, a kindness which in spite of their religious differences he never forgot. The Methodists, like the Roman Catholics, were busy. They sent Colonel John M. Chivington, presiding elder of the Methodist Church in the territory of Colorado, to bless their own log-built chapel. Church collections were small considering that a miner thought nothing of presenting the results of a week's gold panning to his dancing partner.

There was only one murder that first summer and both Tabors were glad when the accused was acquitted. A man named Kennedy had illegally tried to take a mining claim with his gun. Since one of the rightful owners was quicker on the draw, Kennedy fell dead. After the funeral, a miners' meeting found the rightful young owner not guilty.

Augusta did not approve of drinking and told Hod so. Even then he was becoming a good poker player, telling her it would help their business if he fraternized a little in the saloons. In those early days Hod was not actually unfaithful to her but liked to be "one of the boys." Augusta fretted, for she hated to think of their hard-earned money going down the drain. Hod expected her to do all the bookkeeping and post office work, but then as always she loved the man they were beginning to call H.A.W. Thoughtless though he might be at times, there was one consolation: Augusta wore his wedding ring!

Several miners who were leaving the Gulch decided to scrape the floor of a sporting house, and obtained over two thousand dollars from the dirt they ran through their sluice boxes, for the painted ladies were usually paid with gold dust. Oro City was the largest, most rollicking, dirty and ramshackle city in the whole Colorado territory and yet—painted ladies included— surprisingly honest. Of the $5,000 he had made from his claim, Hod gave Augusta a thousand in dust. It was September 20, the time of the year when the aspens turned yellow like the sun. Then wrote Augusta: "I put my wardrobe, what there was of it, in a carpet bag, and took passage with a mule train that was going to the Missouri River. I was five weeks in crossing and cooked for my board."

Maxcy, in his potato sack underwear, was with her, and Hod was to follow later. At last they were going on a visit back to Maine.

Augusta had first met Horace Tabor when she was twenty and he almost twenty-three. Her father had returned early from a Boston-bound trip made to hire new stonecutters for his quarry, for he had been scarcely forty miles from home when two young men carrying stonecutters' tools had boarded the train. Pierce had immediately inquired their destination and upon learning that they were going to Boston in search of work, had engaged them on the spot. Leaving the train at Portland, all three of them had taken the next one back to Augusta.

Horace Tabor was a native of Vermont where, according to his own official biographical notes, he was born November 26, 1830 at Holland, Orleans County, just three miles from the Canadian border. Holland was a quiet, God-fearing farming community where Horace's father, Cornelius Dunham Tabor, was a tenant farmer and part-time schoolmaster.

Sarah, his mother, was strict, frugal and almost fanatically religious. She had little love for Horace, for in him she detected the same weak and indecisive qualities that so marked his father. Her pride and joy lay in his older brother John, who was of a more diligent and persevering nature. Besides, according to Sarah, when John was only twelve he had been *saved*, standing up at Sunday service and dedicating himself to God. As for Horace, even his domineering mother could not instill her own God-fearing instincts in him. If he could get out of attending church on the Sabbath he did so. His truancy from school was only matched by his prowess at fighting.

Horace started his working life as the hired boy at the general store in Holland. For this he received the princely sum of three dollars a week plus all the crackers he could eat. The tall, lanky youth kept the job for a year although he did not particularly like it.

The death of his mother was his excuse for leaving. Although they had never been close Horace insisted that his grief was so great that he could no longer concentrate upon his job.

Then followed a year of idleness. Upon rare occasions he might help his father with the plow but usually he took to the forest instead, where lying under his favorite hemlock he dreamed the pleasant summer days away. When his father and John called him a great lazy ox, Horace only laughed at them. Then fate took a hand in the matter, for Cornelius took a second wife. She proved so unpleasant to seventeen-year-old Horace that he decided to leave home forever. Learning the stonecutter's trade at Quincy, Massachusetts, he traveled the length of three states during the next few years. It was a hard life, with periods of bitter unemployment. Once Horace did become a contractor himself, but somehow he could never keep his money after he had earned it. Even in those early years Horace Tabor had a big heart and was unable to resist a hard-luck story. He had also started to drink.

But Augusta Louise Pierce soon changed all that. She first persuaded her doting father that young Tabor should board with them, and then, with this first step successfully accomplished, set out to thwart his bouts with the whisky bottle. In time, her campaign victorious, she decided to teach him to save.

Hod, as she nicknamed him, was perfectly happy at this stage of his life to be bossed around by Augusta,

for in his subconscious mind she replaced his own domineering mother. After the rough quarry shacks from
which he had been forced to eke out a migratory exist-
ence he found the security of the Pierce home welcome
indeed. He noticed the way Augusta looked at him
over the supper table, and eventually they were holding hands together in the lamp-lit parlor. Never once,
however, did Hod take her for a romantic walk along
the picturesque banks of the Kennebec River or even
to see the new wonder of Maine—the domed State
Capitol built in 1829. Instead he courted her in front
of the kitchen stove, with her chaperoning father always
in attendance.

Strangely enough this state of affairs did not unduly
worry Hod Tabor, for after all, wasn't Augusta his
employer's daughter?

Then one day Hod had suddenly told her he was
determined not to break stones for the rest of his life,
for in his opinion a young man's future lay out West.
He would like to go to Kansas and try his luck. Alarmed
at the prospect of losing the only man who had ever
taken a romantic interest in her, Augusta agreed with
him. She promised that if he liked what he found he
could come back, marry her and they would return
together.

The wedding took place January 31, 1857, in the
Pierces' neat little parlor. As the black-garbed Unitarian
minister closed his book with an air of finality that for
the new Mrs. Tabor could only mean *forever*, she was

silently wondering, with her New England caution, whether she had gotten the thin end of the bargain. In the pause, it was left for her rather boyish bridegroom to take the initiative. Impulsively, he kissed Augusta firmly on the lips. To the surprise of everybody in the room, with the possible exception of her father, the bride pushed Horace away, primly straightened her white velvet wedding bonnet and rubbed off his kiss with the back of her hand. It was an action she would regret for the rest of her life.

Augusta hated what she termed "showing off." In her opinion, she had told her stone-contractor father, a church wedding would be too expensive; she would much rather have the money. So William B. Pierce, admiring thriftiness, gave her two hundred dollars instead, while to his new son-in-law he presented a hundred. Hod told Augusta that as the man of the family he should look after her gift as well. She met this suggestion with a frown, for she thought the two hundred was better left in her own safe-keeping, and if Hod had any sense, he would give her his hundred as well.

Hod nodded his large head, shuffling uneasily, a habit he never overcame. After all, this was his wedding day. He could afford to be generous to Augusta, for had she not agreed to leave the comfort and safety of her father's home to journey with him to far-away Kansas?

William Pierce was glad to see his daughter once again, if a little shocked at the way she had aged, for all the pioneering hardships had left their mark in Augusta's pointed face. For little Maxcy, the greatest thrill was living in a real house. He was a sensible child and remarkably old for his age. In spite of the roisterous environment of the gold camps, he possessed pleasing little manners taught him by his mother. He was devoted to both his parents.

With the thousand dollars she had been given by Hod, Augusta bought 160 acres of land adjoining that which they already owned in Kansas. With a shrewd eye on the opening prairie of the future she believed that land used either for farming or real estate would rise in value. Her family bought her new clothes and outfitted Maxcy, who was particularly proud of his first real homespun vest. In St. Joe, Augusta bought a pair of mules and a wagon to drive them home.

As for Hod, for once he spent his own four thousand dollars wisely, using them to obtain flour and other supplies in Iowa with which to stock his enlarged store in the spring. He even stole an admiring glance at Augusta as she sat in the front of the wagon proudly wearing her new green velvet bonnet. She might not be much of a beauty, he thought, but she certainly had plenty of character.

Back in Oro City, in addition to all her other duties Augusta contracted to convey gold dust for the express office to Denver by horseback. They planned to fool bandits by having Tabor carry a small amount of the gold dust on his own person while Augusta used the first Colorado bank, together with her billowing skirts and many-pocketed flannel drawers, for the bulk. In her opinion not even a bandit would dare to look under a respectable woman's skirts—and among the mining camps respectable housewives were few. As usual, Augusta was right.

That summer when talk of the war that had started between the states was on everybody's lips, the Tabors' business enterprises netted more profits than their mining claim, for the placer gold was nearly exhausted.

Money was of no account then. Ordinary workmen were paid $6.00 per day in gold. They received their pay every night, and the majority spent it before morning. The miners would clean up their boxes, get their gold weighed, go to town, spree all night, and return dead broke in the morning to commence again.

Thus Augusta described life in Oro City at the end of the summer of 1861.

By fall, the sprawling camp that went by the name of Oro City was practically empty. Hearing rumors of a gold boom at Buckskin Joe in South Park on the other side of the Mosquito Range, the Tabors decided to move on, although it was late in the season. Buckskin Joe was named for the prospector who had first found gold there. Later when the town had grown in importance there were those who wanted to call it Laurette, but the threat was never carried out.

The fabulous Phillips Lode that gave the camp its importance was unique, being worked like a quarry. Legend says that a hunter, seeing a deer at close range, had fired and wounded it. Although the creature escaped, the hunter, curious to know if his bullet had found its mark, went in search of blood. This he found and—where the bullet had seared through the sandy top soil—gold as well. Harris the hunter's cabin was soon an Eldorado . . . "Everything in sight filled with the metal, the pure gold—pots, pans, baskets, even a pair of old boots stuffed and stowed away under the bed," according to a contemporary description.

Harris chose for his partner a man named Stancill. They were an extravagant pair, loving amusement. Not content with the three dance halls with which he, in conjunction with his partner, had provided Buckskin Joe, Stancill built a crude theatre in which a Negro minstrel company performed mainly for his own pleasure.

The little community, "with streets regularly laid out and cabins fairly well built," even boasted a newspaper, several quartz mills and a bank. Its impression of permanency appealed strongly to both Hod and Augusta. Perhaps this was why they were prepared to risk the danger of an early snowfall in their eagerness to get settled in before winter. Hod immediately staked himself a number of claims, buying twenty more. Augusta, tired of claims that only turned out—as these also did— to be worthless, quickly opened another store. She had no objection to being their main means of support if her husband would not interfere. His habit of grub-staking penniless prospectors with supplies and tools in return for a share of their findings only annoyed her. Perhaps it was the memory of those early hardships that had made her value money so much, for at Buck-skin Joe she certainly did not practice the Biblical ad-monition "It is more blessed to give than to receive." Augusta ground her teeth as Hod continuously gave, and he never tired of reaching into his pocket to help the needy.

Once more, hard-working Augusta became post-mistress. She was respected even by the "soiled doves," as she called the painted ladies. In any case they were among her best customers, for they always paid their bills. While Augusta served bacon and beans over the counter, Hod often disappeared into some obscure corner to dream just as he had done during his boyhood in Vermont. Storekeeping, like farming, was not for him. One day they had to strike it rich . . . He would hang diamonds around Augusta's neck . . . One day . . . Augusta shrugged her shoulders and laughed when he told her what he would do for her. "I prefer my neck as God made it—without adornment," she told him scornfully. Disdainfully she thought of her soiled dove customers with their diamond necklaces, fancy silk parasols and lace flounces. Even if Hod did find his fortune—which after all these years was extremely unlikely—nobody was going to dress her up like that!

In after years the Tabors spoke little of their days in Buckskin Joe, while contemporary town records hardly mention their presence. The Reverend John L. Dyer, suffering from frostbite in his feet, mentioned later that he "sent to H.A.W. Tabor, our storekeeper—now ex-Senator—and paid him sixteen cents a pound for corn to make hominy . . . a great luxury." Prices were high for everything in the mountains.

"Father" Dyer, as he was known by the miners, was often called the "Snow-shoe Itinerant." Although nearing fifty and gray-haired when during 1861 he had first appeared in Buckskin Joe, he had stopped only long enough to build himself a shelter of boughs before starting his preaching. He knew the language and ways of the miners, having lived among them in Wisconsin and Minnesota, and because of this previous experience the Methodists had sent him as a missionary to the Chippewa country. At Buckskin Joe his street-corner preaching proved popular in spite, as he said, "of two balls a week, a dancing school, a 'one-horse' theater, and many murders." The early Colorado miners could never be pitied for a lack of variety.

"Father" Dyer did not devote all of his amazing energy to the sinners at Buckskin Joe. In winter he visited, on showshoes, the nearly deserted California Gulch, Cache Creek and Gunnison. Once he covered five hundred miles in two months carrying a heavy pack on his back, preaching to congregations who in all that time contributed a total of only $43 to the cause.

From Buckskin Joe he attended the Methodist Conference in Denver, traveling on foot because he hadn't the dollars necessary for a ticket on the weekly stagecoach. Assigned to the Breckenridge Camp and others on the Blue River with an annual salary of $125, he did not complain, although this amount did not begin to cover even the $10 he had to pay weekly for board in so remote an area. His mining congregation was generally friendly, upsetting him only when they borrowed his organ, without asking permission, to provide dancing music. "Very few people realize how little regard people have for sacred things, and what a preacher has to contend with," he grumbled.

At one time, in order to earn money to buy food, Father Dyer carried the mail from Buckskin Joe via California Gulch to Cache Creek for $18 a week. It was not an easy job, carrying a twenty-five pound sack, in addition to express packages, over winter drifts that were sometimes twenty feet deep. Usually he traveled by night when the crust of the snow was firmer. On his day off Father Dyer conducted services at Cache Creek. He carried gold dust for the various camps on the Arkansas, delivering what was later lost to the notorious Reynolds Gang when they held up the Buckskin Coach. The appearance of these ruffians at South Park in 1864 caused a wave of horror and amazement to sweep through the entire mining area. The

stolen treasure, including $40,000 in greenbacks care-
fully protected by silk oilcloth, together with three
cans of gold dust, apparently still lies buried in a mountain cache. "There is no question but that the treasure
is still hidden in the mountains. Though the topography
of the country has been changed somewhat in the last
thirty-three years by forest fires, floods and snowslides,
someone may yet be fortunate enough to find it," General David J. Cook wrote in 1897.

The prosperity of Buckskin Joe came to an overnight
end when the miracle stream of gold abruptly ceased.
Just as suddenly, Stancill, the minstrel lover, departed
to become a spiritualist in Chicago, leaving behind him
$40,000 in debts. His efforts do not appear to have
met with much success in the Windy City, for he
later returned to Denver where he died a pauper.

Of the nearly five thousand who had crowded into
Buckskin Joe in its heyday, now less than twenty were
left. In three years it was nothing but a ghost town.
The Tabors remained, in a state of disillusionment.
Augusta, tired of wandering, wanted a permanent
home. She begged Hod to return to Maine and take
over her ailing father's stonecutting business, but he
absolutely refused. He told her she could take Maxcy,
now a boy approaching thirteen, if she liked, but the
two of them would have to go alone.

When the Printer Boy Lode, a gold mine on the
south side of upper California Gulch, hit a promising
streak in 1868, the Tabors, shaking off their apathy,

moved back. The Printer Boy had been discovered in 1861 but never properly exploited. Once more they opened a store, this time nearly two miles from the southern end of where Harrison Avenue stands in present-day Leadville. Miss Bancroft says, "A group of buildings (now in 1962 mostly gone) about two and a half miles above the same spot was officially designated as Oro. The gulch's inhabitants looked forward to a re-birth of their town." This new Oro City was small compared with the other, having but "several saloons, eating houses and corrals." Together with the Printer Boy, like many a Victorian heroine it soon went into a decline. Bored to death, Hod helped Augusta sort what little mail there was and played poker. She still kept boarders. In 1873 her father, aged 73, died at Augusta, Maine. Augusta made a vow to hold on to her inheritance, modest though it might be compared with the fortune in gold that Hod had dreamed of for so long. The future looked black. Already they were the only operating store left in Oro City. The last saloon had closed. It was fast becoming another ghost town.

Chapter Two

Leadville the Lusty

WHILE California Gulch rested on the laurels of its glorious past, at least one man was busy. His name was William H. Stevens, popularly known as Uncle Billy. He came from Minnesota where he had worked both as a farmhand and iron miner. During the gold rush of '59 Uncle Billy had first appeared in Gregory Gulch, then at South Park, Buckskin Joe and finally California Gulch. In the latter he did moderately well, rewashing old placer claims whose owners had long since abandoned them. He took as his partner Alvinus B. Wood, a metallurgist, whose curiosity was aroused over the heavy black sand and rock that clogged their sluice boxes.

They decided to bring water for hydraulic pressure from the Arkansas River by means of a twelve-mile ditch. Operations began in 1874, being for a time commercially successful and earning between twenty and thirty per cent on the $50,000 that Uncle Billy and his partner had originally invested. Unfortunately, even hydraulic pressure had little effect on the black rock. In June of that year Wood sent samples taken from the south side of the gulch to be assayed, and they were delighted at the results, for the tiresome black rock proved to be valuable silver-lead carbonates with values running from twenty to forty dollars a ton in silver alone!

Sensibly, for two years the partners said nothing about the silver, although they did admit there was lead in the rock. In 1875, while prospecting farther up the gulch, they found a rich silver vein, staking nine claims including the Rock Mine, the Stone and finally the fantastic Iron Silver, destined in its heyday to produce twenty million dollars' worth of silver.

Uncle Billy and Wood started serious mining in the summer of 1876, but unfortunately after hauling the ore by ox-team to Colorado Springs, then sending it by rail to the St. Louis smelter, they found they were still out of pocket. Wood was ready to sell out, which he did in 1877 to Levi Z. Leiter, business associate of Marshall Field of Chicago. At the same time Augustus

Meyer and Edwin Harrison built a smelting and reduction works close to the carbonate mines. Big profits
were expected; once more California Gulch was revital-
ized. Uncle Billy and his new partner found it tough
going for two years, having to battle with opposing
miners, sulphur smoke below ground, and courtroom
lawyers. Prospectors poured back into the gulch; old
sourdoughs who had sat out the years of decline now
believed they were living on a plateau of silver. During
1877, Lake County's output in gold, silver and lead was
to the value of $670,600—the fourth largest in the state.

Names destined to find a place in the history of
America became associated with California Gulch during this great silver boom. One was Meyer Guggenheim,
who arrived to invest his money in the A.Y. and
Minnie mines and quickly turned his attentions to
smelting. With his sons he was to develop the mighty
American Smelting and Refining Company. Another, of
interest to theater patrons of our own era, is Jim Brown,
who was to develop a gold belt in the Little Jonny
Mine and make a million dollars when the price of
silver fell in the panic of 1893. Jim's wife became the
heroine of the 1961 Broadway musical *The Unsinkable
Mollie Brown.*

Once more business boomed. Again the Tabors
moved their store—this time to yet another new Oro
City, often called Slabtown, which had sprung up close
to the smoking ore-smelters. Their new home, more
pretentious than any they had previously known, was

built on the south side of Chestnut Street. Of log and frame construction, it boasted upstairs bedrooms which earned it the name of Tabor's Hotel.

Even the hardworking Augusta could no longer take care of everything, so Hod hired two clerks for the post office. Then he opened a banking department with a large iron safe—so big that it would not fit behind the counter—that was the admiration of all. Everyone wanted to deposit his money in it. More clerks were hired and Hod Tabor, now a prosperous businessman, felt happier than he had been in years.

During the evening of January 14, 1878, eighteen prominent citizens met to select a more suitable name for their new town. They chose Leadville, in honor of the silver-lead carbonates upon which their new prosperity was founded. A town government immediately came into being, and to his own pride and Augusta's satisfaction, Hod was chosen mayor.

He was still generous to strangers and those down on their luck—a much better man than in later years he had credit for being. As for Augusta, a contemporary described her as an "Angel of Mercy, smoothing the pillow of many an ill, homesick and destitute man." Prosperity seems to have made her less penurious. All the same, thought Hod, angel of mercy though she might be to the suffering, they didn't have to live with her. As the years passed Augusta was growing more tart and outspoken. Hod's envious eyes strayed to the beautiful young creatures who had recently invaded the new town, some even owning their own carriages, and he looked critically at Augusta. How sour and dried-up she seemed, almost like a withered apple— and as if to give herself an even more forbidding appearance she had recently purchased a pair of prim pince-nez spectacles.

Both Hod and Augusta were honest people. Prospectors would entrust their monies and valuables to no one else. Augusta enjoyed serving in the store, "weighing out sowbelly and flour, selling picks and shovels, assorting and delivering letters and packages." Sometimes Hod helped, although he preferred to give the orders. At nights he still played poker, when even the professional gamblers who had invaded the new town found him an opponent to be reckoned with. Then one morning fate entered the Tabors' lives.

On Sunday April 21, 1878, two strange German shoemakers-turned-prospectors appeared in the store where Hod was sorting mail, begging for a stake. With his usual good nature he told them to choose what they needed. Augusta was incensed, for she did not like the men's looks, thinking they would never pay for the merchandise. The men, August Rische and George Hook, took $17 worth of supplies, in return for which they agreed to give Tabor a third of their findings.

The mail must have been especially interesting or perhaps a paying customer came in, for neither easygoing Hod nor eagle-eyed Augusta saw one of the men steal a jug of whisky. Hardly a mile from the store the two men sat under a tree to sample it. Then, deciding that one hill was good as another, they started to dig. A day or two later they were back at the Tabors' store for shovels, drills, a hand-winch and blasting powder with which to sink a shaft. Once more Horace obliged. Fortunately, Augusta was away someplace, being an angel of mercy. This time Horace invested another $60 in the former shoemakers.

Early in May, as Augusta was coming downstairs, August Rische came rushing into the store with a handful of ore specimens. He waved them in her face, shouting, "We've struck it! We've struck it!"

It took more than a few rocks in the hands of an excited miner who needed a shave to impress Augusta. Skeptical because of past disappointments, she had long since learned to put her faith only in coal-oil and pies. Drawing herself up and glaring at him from behind her new glasses, she snapped, "Rische, when you bring me money instead of rocks, then I'll believe you."

In less than two months the Little Pittsburgh (as the new discovery was called because Hook had once worked as an ironworker in a Pittsburgh mine) was producing $20,000 worth of ore a week. In fifteen months it had realized $500,000 for Tabor alone. Then Rische and he bought out Hook's interest for $100,000. Immediately the sensible German invested his money in Government bonds before leaving to visit his fatherland. Later Rische, already rich from $145,000 earned in dividends, sold his half interest to bankers for

$265,000. These dividends soon mounted to $100,000 a month. In little under a year Rische's meager grub-stakes had made him half a million.

Tabor was later paid $1,000,000 cash for his share, selling out to David Moffat and Jerome N. Chaffee, Denver banking men. They combined the Little Pitts-burgh with other mines close by under the grand title of Little Pittsburgh Consolidated, selling stock with a capital of $20,000,000. Tabor obtained shares in this new enterprise and made himself another easy million when the stock rose phenomenally from $5 to $30 a share on the New York Mining Exchange. Horace Tabor was now a millionaire twice over—Colorado's first bonanza king. While all these wonderful things were happening, Augusta hung on to her boarders for the rest of the summer. Hod spent less time than ever in the store and by fall they both decided the time had come to sell out. Augusta wasn't sorry, but she shuddered when her husband boasted that he was going to make her a "lady." In her opinion she had never ceased to be one.

Now everything that Tabor touched seemed to turn to gold—or rather, silver. Even those who tried to cheat him lived to rue their deeds. After sinking a shaft on Fryer Hill without finding silver, Chicken Bill Lovell, an old prospector who was a bit of a rogue, gave up when he struck water forty feet below. Early next morning he called upon Tabor with an exciting tale. Just prior to the water episode, he declared, he had made a fabulous ore discovery but lacked the ready cash to drain out the water.

Tabor, always good for a tale, went to have a look, and sure enough, saw plenty of promising ore both in the water and around the shaft top. Although it looked surprisingly like his own Little Pittsburgh ore, he did not question its authenticity, writing out a $40,000 check for Chicken Bill, who couldn't wait to cash it.

The next day Tabor had the mine drained, only to discover that he had been cheated by Chicken Bill, who had liberally salted it with ore and was even then, while under the influence of whisky, boasting of what he had done. Everybody in Leadville was laughing! Augusta was furious with her husband and told him so. Tabor said nothing. Quietly he gave his men orders to sink the shaft another eight feet to encounter the richest body of ore ever found on Fryer Hill. Tabor named it the Chrysolite, and realized $100,000 a month in cash dividends from it for over two years. Later, after incorporating it as the Chrysolite Mining Company, he sold his stock for $45 a share. In all, this salty venture is said to have netted him $3,000,000, and—what to his ego was most pleasing—gave him the last laugh on Leadville, to say nothing of Augusta. There were times now when he even wished he had never married her.

Nothing seemed to stem the Tabor luck. Again Leadville smiled and Augusta shuddered when for $117,000 he bought an almost unproven claim, the

Matchless, which was located near the Little Pittsburgh and Chrysolite Mines. To establish a clear title
to it he would have to spend thousands more. In all
he paid about $150,000 for the Matchless Mine, which
had been discovered by Peter Hughes and six other
poor prospectors in July, 1878, and named for Loril-
lard's chewing tobacco. The Matchless outlasted many
other mines in the area, and although H.A.W. Tabor
did not know it then, would ring down the final curtain
on the Tabor Story.

Along with Tabor, Leadville the Lusty likewise pros-
pered. Happily tagged the "Magic City," it beckoned
the good as well as the bad. "Leadville never sleeps . . ."
ran a story in the local *Chronicle*:

> *The theaters close at three in the morning. The*
> *dance houses and liquoring shops are never shut. The*
> *highwayman patrols the street in quest of drunken*
> *prey. The policeman treads his beat to and fro. The*
> *music at the beer halls is grinding low. A party of*
> *carousers is reeling through the streets. A mail coach*
> *has just arrived. There is a merry party opposite the*
> *public school. A sick man is groaning in the agonies*
> *of death. Carbonate Hill with her scores of brightly*
> *blazing fires is Argus-eyed. Three shots are heard*
> *down below at the old court house. A woman screams.*
> *There is a fight in a State Street casino. The sky is*
> *cloudless. A man stands dreaming in front of the*
> *Windsor looking at the stars—he is away from home.*
> *A barouche holding two men and two women comes*

rushing up Chestnut Street. Another shot is heard down near the city jail. A big forest fire lights up the mountains at the head of Iowa Gulch.

Everyone was welcome in Leadville—everyone, that is, but those unfortunate enough to be Chinese or Indians. Three enterprising Chinese laundrymen from Fairplay met a gory fate. Arriving to set up business, they were shot to pieces and thrown into a deserted prospect hole. Rents were higher than in New York City, stores on Harrison Avenue and Chestnut Street costing between $300 and $500 per month. Bishop— formerly Father—Machebeuf, friend of the early pioneers, sent seven stalwart Sisters of Mercy from Denver to found St. Vincent's Hospital. Theirs was no easy task, for armed desperadoes twice tried to steal the land upon which it was built and pull down the building. A hundred men were recruited "to shoot dead the first man who dares to try to jump the premises."

The Presbyterians likewise had their troubles, for part of their lot was "jumped" so frequently that in the end they decided to take the line of least resistance and build their church in another location.

After hearing that Officer Bloodsworth had escaped on horseback after killing City Marshal O'Connor in a drunken fight, Mayor Tabor appointed a certain Mart Duggan as City Marshall. He proved to be a strange choice—a seasoned killer, with seven notches already on his gun to prove it. Duggan treated guilty and innocent alike, swaggering about Leadville, always longing to pick a fight. One night in a drunken brawl he knocked senseless Rische, Tabor's partner, and dragged him off to spend a cold night in the Pine Street Tombs. Mayor Tabor appealed for his release but was bluntly told, "Close your trap, or you'll be run in, too." Bad as he was, Duggan did gain the reputation of being the only one in Leadville who could instill the fear of the law into the roughnecks.

Thomas F. Walsh, who would live to become a millionaire several times over, built the first good hotel in Leadville, naming it the Grand. His daughter Evalyn Walsh became Mrs. McLean. When William H. Bush, proprietor of the Teller House, Central City, until January, 1879, built the Clarendon on Harrison Avenue, United States senators and other prominent Americans traveled to Leadville for its opening. A newspaper in 1879 quotes Leadville as possessing "19 hotels, 41 lodging homes, 82 drinking saloons, 38 restaurants, 13 wholesale liquor houses . . . 10 lumber yards, 7 smelting and reduction works, 2 sampling works for testing ores, 12 blacksmith shops, 6 livery stables, 3 undertakers, 21 gambling houses (where all sorts of games are played as openly as the Sunday School sermon is conducted), 4 theatres, 4 dance halls and 35 houses of prostitution."

The year 1879 was know locally as "the Reign of the Footpads," for then a man could even lose his pants on the streets in broad daylight. The thieves, called "agents," paid little attention to such ominous warnings as "Get out of town! Stretch your legs before we stretch your neck!" The new school (when it was first built there were those who vehemently protested it to be "inferior in every way to Madame Purdy's House, and a disgrace to a city of 20,000 people") suffered more than its fair share of pilferage. Often the children's outdoor clothes would be stolen from the cloakrooms as they studied inside. Even the dead in the cemetery were not respected, for ghouls robbed newly buried corpses of jewels, and in some instances even of their coffins. Once the *Chronicle* saw fit to warn that three men visiting the city had disappeared.

> *They were taking in the sights, got separated from their friends, and have been seen no more. Their friends know these men were murdered. They were hustled into some dark alley—every alley is dark—or into one of the five hundred dark dens in these dark alleys, killed, robbed, put into a box, and perhaps taken to the City Cemetery and buried in an unmarked grave.*

Panic hit the Magic City when it was learned that the notorious outlaw Jesse James, with his gang including the Ford Brothers, Bob and Charlie (Bob was to shoot Jesse in the back three years later), were working the claim they had staked in California Gulch. Jesse was suspected of robbing two coaches practically on Chestnut Street—until it was discovered that John Fraser, Leadville's captain of police, was the real culprit. However, James and his gang lived quietly during their time in the Gulch, having come to the conclusion that the rich camp itself was well protected. This was true of the big mines, which were always heavily guarded. The owner of the Wheel of Fortune Mine was shot dead when he failed to warn the hired guards of his coming.

In March of 1879 the hungry and destitute, of whom there were many, staged several bread riots which so concerned Governor Frederick W. Pitkin in Denver that he wrote H.A.W. Tabor at once. "The presence of so many people in Leadville, some of whom are idle and destitute, is undoubtedly an element of danger, and even a slight trouble, if not promptly checked, might soon become a serious matter." Pitkin then warned that "not only the lives of good citizens but their property, including merchandise in the stores and money in the vaults of your banks," was in danger. He suggested organizing a "military company."

Tabor loved nothing more than dressing up. At once he called a meeting of Bill Bush, August Rische and other leading citizens to provide several military companies, all supposedly to deal with any Ute Indian uprising, although the unfortunate Utes had been driven over the Continental Divide ages before.

The Tabor Highland Guards comprised sixty-four

men wearing amazing "black doublets, with royal blue and red cord and facings, kilts of royal Stuart style, and stockings dashed with red and green." Augusta upset her husband terribly one evening by poking fun at a guardsman's "sporran of white goat's hair with silver tassels and mountings, a Prince Charlie bonnet ornamented with silver buckle and plume, a Royal Stuart shoulder plaid with silver buckles and *cairn gorn* jewels . . . and *skein dhu* in his stockings." She might just as well have kept quiet, for the Tabor Light Cavalry soon came into being. Horace, now "General" Tabor—a title he loved—and his staff officers wore "black felt hats with a black plume and gold cord, and flashing steel scabbards on belts mounted with gold, and having gold buckles with the monogram of the company." He turned a deaf ear to all the jokes about "Tabor's knees in those damn kilts!"

In addition, the General sported a belt of Russian leather, embroidered by hand (not Augusta's) in gold and valued at $50. On one side of his straight sword was the inscription *General H.A.W. Tabor, C.N.A.*, and on the reverse, *Tabor Light Cavalry*. His epaulets were mounted with a silver star and ornamented with a three-ply genuine gold fringe. The stonecutter from Vermont had indeed come a long way.

According to a contemporary description of the officers' uniform,

The spurs of the privates are plainly formed of brass with steel wheels, while those of the officers

are plated with gold. The uniforms of the officers are
blue broadcloth, trimmed with gold. Their pants are
of light cloth, with broad gold stripes running down
the legs.

It must have been quite a sight when the Tabor Light
Cavalry galloped through Leadville in their glittering
helmets. Their General generously provided them with
club rooms, stables and an armory—the latter opened
with a grand ball at which Horace in his splendid full
uniform quite outshone Augusta, although she is described as attending "in an elegant black silk [dress],
with white lace and magnificent diamond jewelry."
Augusta did not really enjoy the pompous affair, frequently thinking, between dances, of the ten thousand
good American dollars Hod had spent in making himself a general!

Tabor knew how to do things in style. Following
a disastrous fire in which the Coliseum dance hall
burned down, he instituted the Leadville Fire Insurance
Company, with Maxcy, now twenty years old, as its
president. There were three volunteer fire companies:
the Tabor Hose Company with its much admired "four-
wheeled, crane-necked, nickel-plated carriage . . .
a perfect beauty"; the Harrison Hook and Ladder Company (still operating); and the W.H. Bush Hose Company with Maxcy, as its Social President, wearing in
common with the other officers a rather startling straw
hat with special pink front piece.

Among many other concerns in which Tabor had a

finger were two lumber outfits, Tabor, Pierce and Company, and the Little Pittsburgh Company. Both garnered enormous profits. He arranged franchises for his Leadville Water Company, Leadville Illuminating Gas Company and the Lake County Street and Horse Railway, of which he was President. This railway was one of the few Tabor enterprises to be unsuccessful, the three heavy wooden cars being too heavy for the horses to pull up the steep hills.

Bush, who had once taught mathematics at Kalamazoo, became Tabor's right-hand man and finally his partner. He adored racing, and built a half-mile track called the Leadville Trotting and Running Association, which was said to be the best west of the Mississippi. He named his prize gelding H.A.W. Tabor, but bypassed Augusta as a name for its mate. Instead the mare was christened Lily Langtry after the mistress of King Edward VII.

Alone of all the carbonate queens to feel ill-at-ease with the new-found prosperity was Augusta Tabor, now often referred to as the "First Lady of Leadville." Her new house was still little more than a cottage, with clapboards painted brown. There were only six rooms inside and the furniture was simple, the only visible touch of ostentation being a French marble clock and several vases for the wild flowers she still liked to pick. It was hard to have even a summer garden in dry, dusty Leadville although Augusta did manage once to grow yellow poppies and marigolds. Although Tabor

seldom took her with him to the many social functions
he attended, Maxcy was devoted to her. He also appeared very fond of his father. Folks often remarked
that Maxcy seemed the one common bond remaining
between them.

In spite of her husband's indifference, Augusta's
social life was certainly not dull. For the first time in
twenty years she had a home to herself. No longer
were there boarders to cook for or dirty shirts to wash.
Hod had even insisted she should engage a maid. Not
since she was a girl in Maine had she known such
luxury. There might be gambling, dancing and worse
vices to lure the ungodly in Leadville, but the chosen
were not lacking in entertainment either.

There was the Bel Esprit Society and the Leadville
Literary Society, the latter boasting "some of the best
literary minds in the country, including one who wrote
the greater part of Horace Greeley's *History of the
American Conflict*. Augusta once attended a lecture
on Cleopatra's Needle and on another occasion a
performance of "The Boy Stood on the Burning Deck."
She was considered too old to become a member of
the Bicycle Club. Secretly she would have liked to join,
but she declared she would rather be dead than be
seen riding in bloomers. Peeping round the drawn lace
curtains of her little house, enviously she watched the
passing carriages with their happy couples inside. She
often saw the Rev. Dr. Tom Uzzell pass by, looking
"stern and serious as a hard-shelled Baptist" as he

drove "a beautiful span of dark browns." To see him now it was hard to believe that in the first place, before he could come looking for a flock, he had been so hard up that he had borrowed six dollars from an old maid! Even the more fortunate soiled doves drove past in their own carriages, though Augusta wished they would show some good taste by forgetting they had once been her customers, and stop waving their cigars as a greeting.

Along with other respectable Leadville housewives, Augusta was scandalized to be told of the Battle of the Painted Ladies, Mollie May and Sallie Purple, whose houses of sin had enticed many a bachelor and much-married husband. Mollie and Sallie had a terrible row over which of their respective birthplaces was the better, Connaught or Tipperary. Employees and customers took part in the lively gun battle that followed, Madame Purple's entourage being the victors. As the *Democrat* remarked rather tartly next morning, "Both parties are resting on their arms and awaiting daybreak to resume hostilities."

Every branch of the Christian community seems to have been represented in the Magic City. Tabor gave the Protestant Episcopalians $105 to help build their log chapel and presented to the Reverend Uzzell a set of fine crystal chandeliers for his new Spruce Street Methodist Church. Horace liked to spend money and was never miserly. Other Carbonate Kings quickly went through their fortunes. Old Abe Lee, who had first struck gold in California Gulch and later silver at the Dana Mine, squandered two fortunes, ending up a derelict sprinkler for Leadville's "street watering department." In spite of a gala wedding in Chicago and a honeymoon in New York, August Rische, Tabor's partner in good fortune, finished his life as a Denver night watchman. Several enthusiastic women formed their own "Praying Orchestra," whose chief function was to march from one den of iniquity to another where they offered "prayer and song for the salvation of surrounding sinners."

Then Tabor and Bush decided that all Leadville now lacked was an opera house. For weeks the excited residents watched the fine new brick building rise on Harrison Avenue. Next door was the Clarendon Hotel with the Bush-Tabor personal suites linked to the theatre by a catwalk. Phil Golding's Cabinet Saloon, described as the "neatest in the city," was located on the ground floor for the convenience of theatregoers who might need a drink during intermission. Upstairs, Tabor and Bush reigned supreme from behind their large mahogany desks.

Bill Bush, to whom Tabor had leased the new enterprise, engaged an old trouper, Jack Langrishe, as managing director. According to an advance announcement, "all appointments in this temple of amusement are first class in every respect; the scenery, artistic; and under the full flood of gaslight, the cosiest place for lovers of the legitimate drama to throw off the cares of life and yield to the fascinations of music and imagery."

There were 880 seats in an interior that was "handsomely frescoed and furnished with the celebrated opera chairs manufactured by Andrews and Company of Chicago . . ."

With Tabor's new-found wealth and subsequent local fame it was small wonder that he was soon noticed by the politicians. Nominated on the state ticket by the Republicans in November, 1878, he was elected Lieutenant-Governor of Colorado. Delighted, he announced to a somewhat skeptical Augusta that the time had come for them to leave Leadville. They must move to Denver.

"I will never go up these steps, Tabor, if you think I will ever have to go down them."

Proudly Augusta stood at the entrance to the beautiful Henry C. Brown house at Seventeenth and Broadway Streets, Denver. Hod laughed. Wasn't he Lieutenant-Governor of Colorado and a millionaire several times over? "You will never have to leave here," he promised her.

Augusta was entranced with the brick mansion, owned by the man who became famous as the builder of the Brown Palace hotel. She liked the imposing steps leading to the first floor and the lacelike porch running the whole frontage of the house. However, in her opinion, something was missing; something that she considered every fine house should have: green lawns, beds of gaily colored flowers and tall, noble trees. She could still vividly recall the Kansas Prairie lands when Hod and she were young. When she enthusiastically asked if they might make a garden, he laughed again. She was Mrs. H.A.W. Tabor, he told her; she could make ten gardens if she liked. Augusta smiled and impulsively pressed her hand into his in a way she hadn't done for years. Perhaps this lovely home would draw them close to each other again. Her Hod was still as big and strong and virile as he had appeared to her that first day when her father had brought him home for supper—a penniless, unemployed young stonecutter.

In January, 1879, the Tabors rented the new house, purchasing it a month later for $40,000. During their first day of residence, thirty-five curious neighbors called, to be received by a "tight-lipped and nervous" hostess. Sarcastically she remarked, "I would scarcely know how to return the call of the woman next door who arrived in a carriage." However Hod quickly provided her with the most magnificent carriage in Denver, costing $2,000—a replica of the one the President of the United States used in Washington. Such flamboyant luxury only embarrassed poor Augusta the more. In later years she told Flora Stevens, her friend, "La, if we had only had the money that is in that carriage when we began life."

The Tabors' arrival was duly noted by the various

church groups in Denver. Delegations soon began to call, inviting them to join their respective churches. "I suppose Mr. Tabor's and my souls are of more value than they were a year ago," Augusta commented acidly. Finally she settled for Unity Church.

When the snows had gone she supervised her planting, carefully selecting healthy young aspens, elms and pine trees. The plot was suitably landscaped and the tall, rather ugly coach-house pleasantly camouflaged. Even Hod approved, while Maxcy, the pride of Augusta's heart, was elated. He liked living in Denver, where his chances for both social and business advancement were good. Still, Augusta was worried about Hod, for now he seldom spent an evening at home. Night after night she sat alone making her scrapbooks in the great velvet-hung parlor with its heavy mahogany furnishings and ugly brown plush-covered armchairs with lace antimacassars.

She had been resigned to his gambling in Leadville; that had never worried her, for she was broad-minded enough to believe that a man needed some outlet. This present situation was of a more serious nature; even the servants whispered behind her back of the master's carryings-on. It was bad for young Maxcy, whom she was eager to see married into a "good," socially acceptable family, to hear tales of his father's paramours. The servants liked the master to be home, for he was overly generous to them; but Augusta, not used to the management of so large a house, was be-

hind her back called a "shrew" by these same employees because she locked up all the leftovers.

Even the newspapers gossiped about Tabor's love
life. When he was supposed to be away on business,
Augusta, white-faced, would learn that he had heaped
expensive furs and jewels upon the object of his current desires. One reporter insisted that he kept five mis-
tresses, all at the same time, often passing one of them
off as "Mrs. Tabor." Then he picked out—of all people—
a muscular lady named Alice Morgan, by occupation an
Indian Club Swinger! When Alice was not performing
at Leadville's Grand Central Variety Hall she could
usually be found in H.A.W. Tabor's company. Tiring
of her, he next took up with a Miss Willie Deville to
whom he had been introduced in Lizzie Allen's
fabulous Chicago parlor house. So fond did Tabor become of Willie that he couldn't leave her behind in
the windy city. Instead she returned with him to
Colorado, where Augusta soon learned of their affair
and brought the matter to a showdown. Tabor and
Willie purported to part, although secretly they still
managed to meet and even take a pleasure trip to
New York. There the garrulous Willie confided her
love life to a girl friend, who in turn attempted to
blackmail Tabor. For her indiscretion Willie was
promptly given a severance check of $5,000, and Hod
returned to Augusta.

Two years later, Willie told her side of the affair to a
St. Louis newspaper. Augusta was disgusted, although

she did cut out the article and carefully preserve it. As a peace offering Tabor took Augusta on a trip to Chicago, where they purchased real estate. This was something that Augusta, a firm believer in owning land, really did approve of.

Back in Denver, after Augusta had visited her native Maine alone, the Tabors started to quarrel. He wanted his wife to look like a queen while she, rather pathetically, preferred the simple dollar bar brooch containing a strand of his hair to all the diamonds and jewels he had more recently given her. When Tabor left for Leadville to inspect his new Opera House, then nearing completion, Augusta stayed behind in Denver, although she attended the balls given by the Tabor Hose Company in Denver and the Tabor Light Cavalry at Leadville.

November 21, 1879, was opening night at the Tabor Opera House, but the event was rather overshadowed when the Vigilantes decided to lynch two men from the city jail rafters. In just over a month the persistent Langrishe presented nearly twenty melodramas to an audience that did not always appreciate their cultural value. Even the *Chronicle* criticized the "ignorant dolts" who, by their "senseless interruptions, loud laughter and insulting remarks" disturbed those who wanted to listen. The following spring in desperation Bush and Langrishe presented *Othello* with dire results. A certain conscientious Mr. Norris, having witnessed the murder of Desdemona, went straight home after the performance and cut his unfortunate wife's throat. Tabor did not think much of Shakespeare after that, years later being quoted as saying that the dramatist never did much for Leadville.

On July 23, 1880 Augusta was thrilled to share the left-hand box at the Tabor Opera House with ex-President and Mrs. Ulysses S. Grant for the second act of a production called *Ours*. Augusta particularly liked the pleasant Julia Dent Grant, who was very kind to her. She envied them their domestic felicity, which was obvious even to strangers. At the end of the act, amidst much cheering, the two couples left to attend a ball in Grant's honor. It was a momentous day for Leadville. Even the soiled doves had taken a holiday to wave flags and applaud the former President. Tabor had given Grant a friendly Western welcome, slapping him on the back and shouting, "How are you, General?" Grant, rather weary and somber in his black silk hat, was astounded. The *Leadville Chronicle* had been printed on white satin as a souvenir for the ex-President. He liked it so much that he willed it to the Smithsonian Institution, Washington.

The Grants' departure was in a way Augusta's swan-song. Hod, now sporting real diamond shirt buttons as large as dimes, had decided to put her out of his life forever.

The inevitable had happened—the woman reputed to have the most beautiful face in all the west had at last met the fabulous Silver King himself. As long as they lived he would never look with desire at another woman or she at another man. They had first been introduced by Bill Bush sometime between the spring and summer of 1880, when they were respectively twenty-five and forty-nine years old. In March of that year Baby had obtained a divorce from William Harvey Doe on the grounds of his nonsupport and adultery.

Chapter Three

The Belle from Oshkosh

BABY Doe's real name was Elizabeth—"Lizzie" for short—but her brother James first called her Babe or Baby when they were children. Born Elizabeth Nellis McCourt at Oshkosh, Wisconsin, as a young woman she had changed the Nellis to Bonduel after Father Florimond Bonduel, missionary to the Menominee Indians. She declared that he had baptized her in the year 1860 at the home of her parents, Peter McCourt and Elizabeth Nellis McCourt. Baby Doe may well have thought that to be the truth, for the famed Father Bonduel, a friend of her family, had occasionally during the year 1849 and 1850 conducted at her home services for pioneer Catholic families living in Oshkosh. Her mother, who doted on Baby Doe because of the child's great beauty, may easily have invented the fabrication as a means of pleasing the impressionable child. The christening actually took place October 7, 1854, at St. Peter's Catholic Church, Oshkosh, when the Reverend John Cotton officiated.

As an old woman Baby Doe recalled how their mother would say, "Peaches, you're too pretty; don't work too hard. Let your brothers and sisters do the job." As Baby grew up she was soon to realize that her good looks attracted the men of Oshkosh, which made the women hate her. It was something she never forgot, for all her life she distrusted women as friends.

By modern standards Baby's legendary beauty might seem to have been rather exaggerated, for tastes in women's looks have changed. In contrast with the slim silhouette so beloved now, Baby Doe would appear on the plump side. Nevertheless, such plumpness was greatly admired in the 1880's when the curvaceous figure of Jersey Lily (Lily Langtry, the actress, whom Baby somewhat resembled in looks and hair style) was all the rage. Baby's complexion was of a rare, creamy texture. On one occasion gossip was insisting that Baby's envied complexion was painted on with enamel. When another boy teased Peter McCourt about his sister's false face, tempers flared. "It's not true—it's not enameled," shouted Peter, "and I'll take Eddie Adams over to our house and let him feel her face!" Baby's hair was "light golden, rather reddish, and naturally curly." She had a little tip-tilted nose that most men found endearing, and "a round, soft, extremely kissable mouth." From her forebears she had inherited plenty of Irish blarney—and like many another young woman possessed of such beauty, soon gained the reputation for being a "terrible flirt."

In 1866, at twenty-one, her eldest sister Matilda had married a thirty-three-year-old Prussian named Andrew Haben, who by all descriptions must have been a very industrious fellow. At the age of twenty-two, Andrew had been employed by Peter McCourt in his store, but after seven years Andrew opened a similar store down the street, in competition with his former employer and the man who would be his father-in-law. However, the two remained good friends, for the elderly McCourt was generous-minded enough to recognize genuine initiative in the younger man. Baby's German must have improved during visits to her sister's home.

On Election Day, Tuesday April 3, 1877, Andrew, running on the Democratic ticket, became mayor of Oshkosh, moving to a splendid new house on Washington Street. There Baby was a welcome guest at their parties and receptions, learning early how to conduct herself with civic dignitaries and other important guests. She pasted into one of her scrapbooks a clipping about her good-looking brother-in-law, in which he was described as being "deservedly one of the most popular men in the city." He had rich brown hair, a beard and a mustache.

Peter McCourt's finances and business were gradually ruined through six disastrous fires that devastated sections of Oshkosh, but these dire events did not seem to faze Baby Doe.

On one occasion she shocked the ladies of the town by appearing in a figure-skating contest on frozen Lake Winnebago. Up to then only boys had entered, since decorum forbade girls' showing their ankles. Baby's mother seems to have abetted her in the escapade, for it was she who designed the green woolen skating outfit with the much-too-short skirt and neat little fur-trimmed hat. Since she signed her entry blank "E. McCourt," the judges believed the competitor to be one of her brothers until her name was called to perform. A gasp of horror went up from the watching crowds, but this did not worry Baby McCourt, who was a natural exhibitionist. She skimmed over the ice as if she hadn't a single care in the world—and of course won the contest.

A turning point in the life of the Belle of Oshkosh came in the spring of 1876. That day she wrote with trembling heart in her scrapbook, "I MET MY LOVE ON THE STREET, April 3, 1876." Her love turned out to be William Harvey Doe, Jr., whose family called him Harvey or Harve.

Shy and good-looking, with hair almost as fair as

Baby's, Harvey Doe fell into the unfortunate category of Mother's Boy. He was also the adored brother of five sisters. The Doe family were prominent Methodists and Congregationalists, his uncle being the Reverend F.B. Doe, and the entire world of Mama Doe collapsed the day her beloved Harvey came home glowing with admiration for "that fast Baby McCourt." She declared that the girl destined to be her future daughter-in-law was nothing but a "Romanist and Papist." To add insult to injury, Democrat Andrew Haben, Baby's brother-in-law, had defeated Harvey's Republican father in the April 3, 1877, Oshkosh election for mayor. The harder Mama Doe tried to break up the courtship the more determined did Baby become to take Harvey away from her, overlooking the fact that he was such a weakling.

As for Mrs. McCourt, she was quite taken with her favorite daughter's choice. When Harvey came visiting in the evenings she thrilled to his "lovely voice and the way he played the piano." Firmly she told Baby to take no notice of what Mama Doe was saying. The McCourts still had their pride, despite the McCourt reverses in fortune. When Harvey plucked up courage to propose, Baby lost no time in accepting.

Papa Doe liked Baby from the beginning—but then all her life men enjoyed her company. In the spring of 1877 the engagement was finally announced, and Baby discarded forever all notions of going on the stage. Mama Doe fumed, fretted and was taken with make-believe heart attacks, but nothing could shake her darling Harvey from taking as his bride the prettiest girl in town. Harvey was flattered when the other young fellows envied him his good luck in winning her hand. Mrs. McCourt scraped and saved to buy her daughter a beautiful wedding gown and to pay for a reception that even the standoffish Does could not criticize. Just three days before the wedding, Harvey, of his own accord and without even consulting his mother, joined the Roman Catholic Church.

Baby was twenty-two and her groom twenty-three on the lovely summer day of June 27, 1877, when they were married by Father James O'Malley in St. Peter's Church, Oshkosh. Both families were so well known that it seemed half the town was there. All through the service and subsequent reception Mama Doe sat looking glum and sad, as though she were losing her son forever; but when Mr. and Mrs. William Harvey Doe, Jr., left for Central City, Colorado, following the reception she made a mental vow to follow in their wake as soon as possible.

Chapter Four

The Miners' Sweetheart

W HEN Baby Doe first saw the mountains, she had an inexplicable feeling that her destiny was bound up in those distant granite fortresses, and the few days' honeymoon spent at the American House gave the wide-eyed girl from Wisconsin a glimpse of another world of wealth and everything that went with it. She envied the wives of the rich bonanza kings in their splendid satins and jewels, and thought it romantic that the Grand Duke Alexis had been given a ball in that very hotel only five years ago. Baby Doe held her head high, for she was sure Harvey would be just as rich as the other husbands, and provide her with every conceivable luxury.

They traveled by train to Black Hawk, where they expected to be met by Harvey's father, "Colonel" Doe. Instead, he had left a note with the depot master telling them to take the omnibus stage up to Central City, a mile's drive away, where he would be awaiting them.

The "Colonel" had no right to his title, for during the Civil War he had paid a substitute to represent him on the field of battle while he waxed rich in Colorado. Afterwards he gave up mining and retired to lumbering interests in Oshkosh, only making periodic visits back to Central City as superintendent of the Sierra Madre Mining Company. In Oshkosh he had become very civic-minded. He was bigger than Harvey, bluff and gay. Baby Doe admired his business acumen more than she did his choice of a wife.

Driving up to Central City was not so appealing as Baby had dreamed it would be. The trees had long since been felled; ugly piles of rubble and ore spewed out over the once lovely hillsides. The little towns of Blackhawk, Mountain City, Central City, Dogtown and Nevadaville seemed to be stacked one on top of the other. They made Baby Doe giddy just to look at them. She pressed Harvey's large hand with her own.

Central City itself seemed surprisingly permanent, with new brick buildings dating from 1874. In that year, as in the preceding one, Central City had been swept by fire. The "Great Fire" had been started by joss sticks in Chinese Alley, which resulted in the near-lynching of the unfortunate man responsible for the conflagration. Baby liked the warmth of the new red bricks and the well-laid stonework in the various retaining walls. Cornish miners (known locally as "Cousin Jacks" because they seemed related to everybody else in their native Cornwall) had brought their stone-building skill over from the old country. They also possessed fine voices and were members of the various "cultural" choral groups with which Central City was particularly blessed. It was little wonder that a real Opera House was being built. Because of her love for anything theatrical this last piece of news greatly interested the new bride.

Colonel Doe was walking alone down the hill from the Teller House when Harvey and Baby arrived; Mama Doe was apparently still recovering from the shock of the wedding. Good-humoredly he explained that he could not meet them at Black Hawk as he was waiting to have a brake put on the buggy that had been shipped especially from Wisconsin. Later that day when it was fixed he drove the eager young couple to see the Fourth of July Mine, in which Baby was sure their fortune lay hidden.

Colonel Doe and Benoni C. Waterman, who also had a twenty-stamp quartz mill at Nevadaville, had bought the undeveloped mine jointly in 1871. Waterman was quite agreeable to the Colonel's leasing his share for two years during which time the latter promised to sink the existing shaft another 200 feet. If this resulted in the ore harvest they hoped for, then, after the first year, Harvey could buy out Waterman's interest for $10,000, or $15,000 the second. If the ore was not forthcoming Waterman was to be given the right to sell his half interest. The Colonel was prepared to present most of his own profits to Harvey, declaring also that if his son showed promise he could then have the half share outright in his own name. Baby Doe was even more elated at this good news than her husband.

Colonel Doe introduced his son and daughter-in-law to various people in town including Joseph Thatcher, the goateed president of the First National Bank, and Bill Bush, proprietor of the Teller House.

A contemporary description of the Teller House parlors and bedrooms, taken from the Central City *Register*, gives some idea of their magnificence:

> The parlors are perfect marvels of elegance. They are elaborately furnished with the latest approved styles in walnut and damask, and carpets of the finest Brussels. The piano—a Knabe square grand—has great volume and richness of tone, its strings clear and resonant as the finest Steinway. All the sleeping rooms, to the number of ninety, are tastefully fitted up with all the essential conveniences.

Fortunately in our own era the Teller House has been faithfully restored to delight the eyes of future generations. It did not suffer the fate reserved for the equally historic Clarendon Hotel in Leadville or the once magnificent Windsor Hotel, Denver.

Thatcher and Bush, both still in their thirties, promised the beautiful Baby Doe that they would be only too glad to advise her husband on business matters after the Colonel's return to Wisconsin. Mr. and Mrs. W. Harvey Doe, Jr., promptly moved into a cottage on Spring Street where Baby kept busy for a few days arranging her wedding presents and other knickknacks beloved of the Victorian bride. Finally "Colonel" Doe departed for Oshkosh. At last they were alone.

Unfortunately Baby realized almost the same day what it was really like being married to a Mother's Boy, for Harvey hated making his own decisions. He procrastinated over everything, so that not until August 18 was the agreement with Waterman drawn up, although they had arrived in Central City early the previous month. At long last, on September 6 she managed to inveigle Harvey to the Court House to register it, watching with much relief as her husband signed, "W.H. Doe by W.H. Doe, Jr."

If Harvey had failed to realize the importance of being alert in this Colorado gold town, she had not, for visits to Bush and Thatcher had taught her much. His mother had always done all of his thinking so that he now expected his wife to do the same. Baby Doe, bursting with health, vitality and her first taste of independence, began to find annoying that very shyness she had admired so much in their early courting days. The truth was beginning to dawn upon her: she had married a weakling.

Hearing tales of how in these vigorous mountain towns others had been cheated out of their holdings, Baby Doe decided that if she was to be Harvey's mouthpiece she would have to confide in somebody. Again she chose Thatcher, taking him an ornament she had made out of raffia as a gift. Thatcher was both touched and amused. He promptly gave orders for it to be hung below the cast-iron holder of the bank's magnificent gas jet chandelier where it remained for many years.

In return he gave Baby Doe some sound business advice: "Get working on the mine before the snow comes."

Unfortunately for Harvey Doe, the ore samples from his new shaft were disappointing and the assayer told him that he was wasting good money even to test them. The Cousin Jacks working for him were equally discouraging. A very downcast bridegroom went home to his Baby Doe. Almost in tears, he blurted out his story of failure. What would they do when the money his father had left them was gone? How would they pay the miners? Baby comforted him, like a little boy; then she thought of some of the stories told her by Thatcher. Why not sink another shaft? After all there were five hundred feet along the claim. Harvey meekly shrugged his shoulders. He was all ready to give up and go home to his mother.

Baby petted him some more. Being bored in the cottage, why couldn't she help him at the mine? She had no friends and missed her own family. He could look after one shaft while she ran the other. Surely Mr. Thatcher who liked her would lend them the money.

And Mr. Thatcher did. He admired Baby Doe for not giving in. It was good to come upon such a beautiful young woman who was not afraid of hard work. The new shaft was sunk and Baby Doe, dressed like an ordinary Cousin Jack, personally ran the horse-drawn whim. Not only the ladies of Central City, but some of their menfolks as well, were incensed at her lack of femininity. Even Bill Bush, as the respectable father of a growing daughter, Antoinette, found Mrs. Doe's friendship no longer acceptable. No lady would dress like an ordinary miner. From now on he too would cut her in the street. Besides there was much disgusting talk of women fighting for their rights. The dreadful Lucy Stone had come all the way from Boston to address the women of Denver, Golden and Central City, and even though Baby Doe did not attend, the very fact that she was doing a man's work showed her to be sympathetic to their cause. The reformer Lucy Stone had already won a name for herself as a lecturer for the American Antislavery Society. Although she did not think it harmful to her cause in 1855 to marry a mere man (Henry B. Blackwell, himself an acceptable abolitionist), she reserved the right to keep her maiden name. In 1870 she founded and edited the *Woman's*

Journal, a periodical advocating women's suffrage that had a life-span of almost fifty years.

October came—Baby Doe's first Colorado fall—and she gloried in its golden beauty. About this time a man writing in *Town Talk,* a short-lived Central City publication, under the pseudonym of "The Mining Reporter," said,

> *I next reached the Fourth of July Lode, a mine which has not been worked for several years but started up some months ago under the personal supervision of the owner, Mr. W. H. Doe and his wife. The young lady manages one half of the property while her liege Lord manages the other. I found both at their separate shafts managing a number of workmen, Mr. Doe at his which is 70 feet, and his wife who is full of ambition, in her new enterprise, at hers which is sunk 60 feet. This is the first instance where a lady, and such she is, has managed a mining property. The mine is doing very well and produces some rich ore.*

This only added fuel to the flame. Not only were the respectable wives, mothers and spinsters of Central City shocked beyond words but so were many of the town's painted ladies. More than one of the latter told her evening partner that "hussies like that Mrs. Doe should know their proper place." A respectable wife saw fit to write a long letter to Mama Doe, telling of the carryings-on of her daughter-in-law who dressed like a man all week and a princess on Sundays.

Mama Doe could hardly contain herself as she read on. Her daughter-in-law who should be home looking after *her* Harvey was instead cavorting around the countryside on a spirited horse named Pet with the grandest sidesaddle in the city. And her outfit—a black serge riding habit with a high white stock. Her Empress Eugénie hat was covered with ostrich plumes. . . . The only thing good and ladylike in her favor was that she did wear gloves.

Poor Harvey's Mama. She couldn't pack her trunk fast enough. Together with her husband and two of her daughters she set out posthaste for Central City. Only a severe attack of the shingles had prevented her from coming earlier.

Baby was far from happy about her mother-in-law's pending visit, never having quite forgiven her opposition to the wedding. As for Mama Doe, the first thing she did upon arriving in Central City was to inform Harvey quite definitely that his bride was no housekeeper. In fact, the cottage was a disgrace. Instead of telling his mother to mind her own business; that his wife could not work at the mine and put as much time as she would like into her home, he simply repeated to Baby what his mother had said. Immediately her Irish temper flared, and she vowed she would not stop in the same place as Mama Doe. Harvey sulkily shrugged his shoulders. He loved his mother and he loved his wife.

Suddenly Baby had an idea. Since houses were so hard to find, why didn't they let Mama Doe have the cottage? They could move down into Black Hawk. Colonel Doe was pleased with the idea, thinking that Baby was being very kind and dutiful. Secretly he had admired the way she had pushed Harvey into opening up a second shaft and worked it herself, for "Colonel" Doe had no rosy illusions concerning his son. In his opinion, Baby, with her pluck and initiative, was just the right wife for Harvey. Quickly he helped the younger Does find rooms over a brick store on Gregory Street. The new apartment had long, attractive windows with rounded tops which Baby said jokingly reminded her of a church.

Forbidden now to work at the mine, Baby Doe looked around for something else to occupy her time. Keeping their rooms tidy now was no problem; for in spite of her mother-in-law's accusation she was really a very methodical person. She did not particularly like to cook, but when she was careful, she was very adept at it. When the weather was good in Black Hawk she preferred to take long walks picking wild flowers to press for her new scrapbook.

The people of Black Hawk, even the women, were more friendly than those of Central City. There were one or two snobbish families who still would not speak to her, but the miners—sometimes in whispers so loud that she overheard—called her the "Miners' Sweetheart." Of the women, she liked best a certain Mrs. Richards, better known as "Cousin Jenny," who would give her fragile yellow poppies from her own little patch of garden on the hillside, always telling her, "You are like a seraph—an angel." Baby, lonely for her own folks in Wisconsin, loved such flattery.

Another favorite calling place was the Sandelowsky, Pelton and Company men's clothing store on Gregory Street, four doors away from her own. Even the building fascinated her, for it had a delightful pointed brick fringe along the front, looking like a giant chain of Christmas pennants. Outside were dummies' heads stuck upon clothes stands. The dummies, one of which was complete with a fashionable mustache, wore hats, ties, shirts and coats. Their empty sleeves swayed garishly in the breeze.

The store, which also sold boots and shoes, was run by two handsome young Jews named Jacob Sandelowsky and Sam Pelton. Jacob, with his flashing black eyes, dark brown curly hair, mustache and particularly long fingers, was the best-looking man Baby Doe had ever seen. His reputation as both gambler and ladies' man did not unduly worry Baby Doe, for since coming to Colorado she had learned that gambling was part of the mountain life. Understandably Jacob and Sam soon noticed Baby Doe and it was not long before they were on speaking terms. Like many wives, she liked to choose her husband's clothes. Christmas was coming. Would they help her choose Harvey a present?

It was not long before she had learned that Jacob had been born on Christmas Day in his native Poland, at the age of fifteen emigrating with his parents to

Utica, New York, going with them into the clothing business. In 1870, at eighteen, he had arrived in Central City, where he entered the clothing business with Abe Ratchofsky as his partner. The firm was dissolved in 1874 and Jake opened another store in Black Hawk with Sam Pelton. Baby Doe was suitably impressed. With body erect and head tilted to one side, she daintily picked her way home to get Harvey's supper. Jake, feeling strangely lightheaded and gay, watched her go. He had known all sorts of women, but this one was different. She had beauty, a brain and plenty of pluck. Why, he thought as he watched her turn into her own doorway, did she have to be married?

Baby Doe sometimes asked herself the same question, for marriage to Harvey was sadly disappointing. Even though the Fourth of July was starting to pay, she was a long way from being the wife of a millionaire. As for Harvey, he spent more time with his mama than he did with her. On October 25 Baby sadly watched Elias Yutsey make his last run down the hill as driver for the stage line from Idaho Springs to Central City. As the stage coach rushed past in a cloud of dust Baby couldn't help thinking that she was watching the end of an era.

At first Harvey had no objection to Baby's friendship with Jake and Sam, for he, too, found them good company. Usually Harvey was shy and self-conscious with even his own sex, but these two young men were carefree and jolly, and at Baby's suggestion he invited them

for Christmas dinner on what was also the occasion of
Jake's twenty-sixth birthday. To Baby's gift Harvey
pinned the message:

> *A merry Christmas from Bub.*
> *My own my true one Lizzie*
> *Accept this token as only a*
> *partial gift*
> *From the man whome loves*
> *and worships you.*
> HARVEY.

Baby Doe stayed up nearly all the previous night
preparing the goose. Mama Doe sniffed and remarked
that it was a pity her daughter-in-law did not take as
much time perfecting all of her meals. The goose must
have tasted good, for Sam and Jake continued to be
regular visitors to the young Does' home, even teach-
ing them how to play poker. First of all, however, Jake
made Baby promise never to play in public. She laughed
at the mere suggestion. She had ruined her reputation
enough, working in the mine and riding her horse on
Sundays, without committing the further indiscretion
of playing poker.

Jake, Baby and Harvey were on such good terms that
Baby was able to indicate in her scrapbook "Feathers
out of my dead bird's wing that Jake and Harvey
buried on the mountain back of Jake's store." Underneath a posy of yellow flowers she wrote, "Picked these

flowers near my bird's grave, the day that Jake showed me its grave."

These were happy days for Baby Doe and, strangely enough, for Harvey also, for he enjoyed Jake's company as much as she. His marital relationship with Baby improved; they did not quarrel so frequently. For the next few weeks she was very loving towards him. The Does attended a New Year's hop (dance) at the Black Hawk Club held January 12 in Marsh and Buffington's Hall, which brought Baby nostalgic memories of the McCourt Hall at Oshkosh. Since she and Harvey had started courting she had not danced once, for his mama had never allowed him to learn. At the hop she was partnered by Jake—and what a handsome couple they made! If others in the room were talking, Harvey did not seem to mind.

The two clothiers had tickets for the four of them to see the opening performances at the grand new Opera House on March 4 and 5, and what wonderful nights they were! Baby was particularly taken by the massive chandelier with its hundred glittering gas jets. The drop curtain was painted with a scene on the Rhine including a romantic balcony and a fairytale-like castle. As Baby Doe sat in the crowded theatre she pressed Harvey's hand, but deep in her heart she was thinking of Jake.

The Fourth of July continued to pay, as did Colonel Doe's Wood Mine. Then, in May of 1878, the story changed. As the Cousin Jacks said, both mines went "in cap," their golden veins running out. Besides, silver had been discovered in fantastic quantities at Leadville. Many residents of the Gulch of Gold of which Black Hawk and Central City formed part were seriously talking of moving there. This was ironic, for on May 21 an event of much local importance was taking place: the Colorado Central Railroad had at last linked Black Hawk with Central City. It seemed to Baby that the trains were roaring right through her bedroom, as they passed over a trestle bridge built literally beside it.

Baby attended the grand parade in Central City chaperoned by her three beaux. There was every conceivable amusement to see and hear, from the firemen's tournament to the McDaniel Brass Band. One of the competing firemen, William E. Roberts of Denver, noticed the beauteous Mrs. Doe that day as he talked to his friend Andy McFarlane. He never forgot what he saw. "When a vision of loveliness glided by, I asked Andy who the fairy was," he recalled years later when the fairy had become the Silver Queen.

Said Andy, "All I know is that her name is Mrs. Doe. That man dancing with her is a prominent gambler and quite a lady-killer."

The year before, Jake had taken a certain Rosa Allen, a dance hall girl from Black Hawk's Shoo Fly, for a trip to Denver, staying with her at the élite American House—something neither Harvey nor Baby Doe knew.

Meanwhile all Central City was still talking about fabulous Leadville and of penniless prospectors' becoming millionaires overnight. Baby Doe heard several different versions of how a certain grocer named H.A.W. Tabor had already reaped a fortune from the Little Pittsburgh mine. Although gold had made Central City famous throughout the world, its inhabitants' thoughts were now mostly of silver.

Colonel Doe was the second man from Central City (Nathaniel P. Hill, whose Black Hawk smelter even had a telephone, was the first) to head for the new silver strike. The Colonel chose Mill City (now Dumont), four miles West of Idaho Springs, as his scene of operation. A house was soon built for Mama Doe and the girls, and needless to say, Baby was delighted to see them go. Harvey was left to cope with the failing Fourth of July, although his father, doubtful of his son's capabilities, frequently drove over in his buggy to supervise things.

All that summer Baby had enjoyed Jake Sandelowsky's favors, and although Harvey was usually with them, people still gossiped over the friendship. There was no doubt that Baby was fascinated with the handsome, curly-haired gambler or that their affair had passed the stage of friendship. Under a few pressed blue gentians she wrote in code, "Jake gave me these September 25, 1878, the night of the festival in his store when we sat on the school house steps together. He kissed BT three times and oh! how he loved me and he does now."

Once more the Belle of Oshkosh was emerging as something of a local *femme fatale*.

Under Jake's photograph she placed a few yellow flowers. This particular picture emphasizes his handsome gold watch chain and the very pronounced veins on his hands. Around him she pasted poems with such varied titles as "I Love Thee," "Possession," "The First Meeting" and "Dreamers."

Harvey, round and pasty-faced in his photograph, appears, in spite of his important-looking top hat, a poor second beside the dashing Jake. Next to his picture his wife stuck the words, "A wound from the tongue is worse than a wound from the sword; for the latter affects only the body, the former the spirit—the soul."

Suddenly, on November 18, 1878, Colonel Doe decided to close the mine. (Ironically, during the 1880's the Fourth of July made a fortune of more than $200,000.) It was then that Baby realized that her confidence in Harvey's making a fortune had been only wishful thinking. Her pride was further hurt when her husband took a night job in the Nevadaville mill of Herbert Waterman, son of that same Benoni C. Waterman who owned half the shares of the ill-fated Fourth of July.

When Jake told her she could become superintendent of the ladies' department of his Central City store, Baby Doe quickly accepted. It would not be hard work, he assured her, and the salary was good. She immediately asked Bill Bush at the Teller House to find rooms for herself and Harvey. Bush hesitated, saying that he had nothing suitable at the time, although on November 21 he was able to offer them two rooms with fire at $18 weekly. By that time the Does had found other accommodations in the Mueller Block on Eureka Street, Central City. The Sandelowsky, Pelton and Company store in that neighborhood was conveniently close.

While Harvey conveniently worked nights, Jake and Baby Doe became lovers. They had clandestine meetings near the railroad trestle that precariously spanned Packard Gulch at Mountain City. Baby indiscreetly pasted a picture of the trestle in her scrapbook, writing underneath, "Meet me, my darling, at ten."

Harvey's fortunes ebbed still further; he was unhappy at his new job, in debt to the First National Bank and homesick for his mother, while Baby Doe was glad enough of Jake Sandelowsky's interest. Not only was he her lover but, what was more important, he helped out with their finances and many times paid for the groceries.

That winter Bush left the Teller House for prospering Leadville where he planned to erect the Clarendon Hotel. Baby, now quarreling frequently with Harvey and tiring of Central City, was pleasantly surprised when Jake presented her with a valuable gift of jewelry. With it came a receipted bill dated March 11, 1879, from Thomas Kilpatrick, Jeweler, New York, to show that it was genuine. Although she clipped off Jake's name she did post the telltale piece of paper into her bulging scrapbook:

Three diamonds..$1,185.
Two solid gold puff bracelets.....................$ 250.
One shaking solid gold cross.....................$ 50.

She had never had such a gift, and common sense told her that a married woman ought not to accept expensive trinkets from a man who was not her husband. Besides, she had discovered that she was going to have a baby.

When Colonel Doe visited the Teller House on March 7, Harvey asked for cash to open up the Troy lode on Quartz Hill. Telling the Colonel of Baby Doe's condition, he declared that it did not appear right that he, the only son of Colonel Doe, should continue to work as a laborer.

It is interesting to surmise why Colonel Doe had allowed him to do so in the first place. Did he think it would teach him to stand on his own two feet and make a man of him? Or was it to spite Mama Doe, in whose affections he had for years been supplanted by Harvey? Whatever it was, the Colonel gave Harvey a good dressing down. He reminded him that in 1859, the year of the big fire in Oshkosh, it had not been beneath his own pride to work as a common laborer in Colorado.

Harvey cursed his father and went drinking. The next morning he confronted Baby with the story he had heard from some drunken miners, that the child she carried was not his but Jake Sandelowsky's. This was too much for Baby's Irish temperament. Picking up an ore specimen, she threw it at Harvey and cut his head open. Filled with rage, Harvey left the house, from which weeks later he was still missing. During that time she turned to Jake for encouragement and support.

Her parents, learning of their daughter's desertion, insisted that she should come home to Oshkosh, which she did, staying until Colonel Doe effected a reconciliation with Harvey. The latter had returned to his mother for consolation; she could not understand her husband's eagerness to reunite their son with "that hussy" again.

Upon her return to Central City, Harvey apologized sheepishly to his wife. They had both done wrong; he was sorry for what he had said about the expected baby. He would try to make it up to both of them. With a final lecture to his son and daughter-in-law, the "Colonel," having found them fresh rooms, returned somewhat relieved to his new silver holdings and the furious "Mama" Doe.

For a month they were happy; even some of the old magic returned to their relationship.

On July 13, Baby Doe's first child, a son, was stillborn. Harvey had been so overcome with fright at his prospective fatherhood that Jake had had to run for the midwife—while some sources maintain that he even paid for her services.

In her scrapbook, but this not in code, Baby Doe

wrote, "My baby boy had dark, dark hair, very curly, and large blue eyes."

Colonel Doe, minus Mama, rushed over to help them through this new crisis, helping Harvey arrange for the infant's burial. He was bitterly disappointed at losing his grandson. In spite of all the gossip both Harvey and his father believed the child to be truly a Doe.

Under more pressed flowers, Baby Doe sentimentally recorded, this time partly in code, "Flowers from my baby's grave given me by Love Sunday evening, September 28, 1879, my sweet baby boy."

Whether "Love" referred to Harvey or Jake, only Baby knew, and she carried the answer to her grave.

Meanwhile the fortunes of Jake and his partner Sam Pelton were increasing. It was decided that Jake would open a new branch of the business on the ground floor of the wonderful Opera House which Tabor the Bonanza King was building in Leadville. To clear the lot for its erection on Harrison Avenue, Hod and Augusta's little house had been moved to a new site at 116 Fifth Street.

Introduced to him by Bill Bush during a quick visit he had made to look over Leadville, Jake had been much impressed by the "fabulous" H.A.W. Tabor. His timely move into the new store allowed him a share in the fanfare of publicity attending the grand Opera House opening.

Then, surprisingly, Jake asked both Baby and Harvey Doe to visit him in the suite of rooms at its rear. This was not the psychological time for Harvey to be visiting a successful rival, for once more he was in difficulties, having lost his new job as a miner at the Bobtail tunnel. He had taken to drinking heavily again, and was deeply in debt.

Deciding to try their luck in Denver, the Does left Central City forever. Baby was not sorry, for with the exception of her brief idyll with the handsome gambler-clothier, she had not been happy there.

In Denver her life with Harvey went from bad to worse, for half the time she did not even know where he was. On March 2, 1880, accompanied by Edward Newman, a policeman, she followed Harvey to the scarlet domains of Madame Lizzie Preston's parlor house on Market Street. Her discoveries were such that two days later she filed a suit for divorce, charging not only adultery but also nonsupport.

On March 19, Denver's prettiest "injured wife" testified tearfully that she had had to sell not only their furniture in order to support them both, but her jewels and clothing too. The judge was sympathetic, and Baby Doe, her head tilted to one side, tripped out of court a free woman.

Difficult as their brief married life had been, in his heart poor Harvey did not want to lose her. Pathetically he penned a childlike plea to his parents to "look into this matter this sad sad affair."

The letter read:

THE MINERS' SWEETHEART

American House,
Denver, Col.,
Mar. 29 1880.

My Dear Father & Mother

You have of corse herd before this of my sad sad loss in loosing my darling Babe I am heart broken about it I shal go crazey about it I know I shal for my dear Father & Mother it was not my fault that I went into that parlor house. Let me tell you all about it and then I hope you will not blame me there is a man in this town who was trying to sell my mine for me. We had been looking all over town for a man who he said he could sell it to so we hunted all over for him so this man said let us look in Lizzie Preston's for him I told him I did not go into such places as that Well he says if you want to sell your mine to this man we have got to find him tonight for he is going away in the morning so I told him if he would not stay in there I would go in and right out again So I went in and who should be a cross the street but Babe and saw me going in there I did not stay I did not stay in there only long enough to see if that man was in there just as I was going to go out Babe came there and caught me and she did act like a perfect lady and conducted herself so nicely in such a place as that. Now my dear Father & Mother do not blame me I went in there on business of great importance to me I can assure you. I was so hard up I did not have any money nor nothing to eat in the house and I thought if I could find this man I might get some money from him to help me out I did not

go in that place with any bad intentions   no   no I
love my darling wife babe to much ever to disgrace
her in that manner   I have been as true to her as any
man could be to his wife so I went into that parlor
house thinking I might get some money to help us
along in the world   God only knows I have had a hard
time of it for the past two years trying to get along
in the world and get ahead so I could get a home
for us that we might live happy and enjoy ourselves.
Even my own Father has worked against me and
wherever he could hinder me from making money he
has done so. I hope and sincerely pray my dear par-
ents you will not blame me and do try and get babe
to come back to me for she is all I have got in this
world   do try and pursuade her to come back to me
for with out her I am a miserable man and am nearly
crazey abot the affare I hope you will do all in your
power to persuade her to come back to me and do
not blame me for I did not do any harm at all   Babe
has got a piece of Property which I gave her a year
ago which she can sell and I sincerely pray and hope
she will come back to me. Hoping now my dear par-
ents you will look into this matter this sad sad affair
is the ernest wish of your
Loving Son
HARVEY

Baby's connection with the Doe family was now almost severed, for there remained only the matter of
the disposal of her mining interests. Colonel Doe, who
still liked Baby and was genuinely sorry to learn of

the divorce, agreed to buy the three Central City claims that Harvey had given her, the Muscatine, Troy and Troy Number 2. The Colonel realized he was getting off lightly, for if Baby had claimed alimony it would have been his money that paid it. Harvey had none of his own. With the proceeds from the mining sale, Baby Doe happily set out for Leadville—and Jake.

Life in the Cloud City was every bit as exciting as she had been led to believe. She lived at a boarding house while Jake lodged at 303 Harrison Avenue. His business, Sands, Pelton & Company (he had now fashionably Americanized his name to Sands) was prospering. He had even joined the Tabor Light Cavalry. Baby Doe stuck into her scrapbook several party favors and invitations to balls addressed to "J. Sands and Lady."

One wonders why they did not marry at once, for Jake was very much in love with her. Perhaps his gambling made her wary of matrimony. On Jake's part, it is surprising that if he wanted her so much he did not propose marriage immediately, for there were plenty of other admirers only waiting to step into Harvey's vacated shoes. One such gentleman was a certain T.B. Corrigan who on June 18, 1880, sent her a letter written on Palmer House (Thoroughly Fire-Proof) stationery. It was simply addressed to "Mrs. Elizabeth B. Doe, Denver, Col.," and subsequently redirected to her new Leadville address.

Corrigan wrote:

Dear Friend —
I know of your domestic trouble, and to be brief,
would simply ask you to sit down and write me as
you would to the best friend you have. If I should
have the pleasure to hear from you and you desire
it, I may write you a more interesting letter.

Obviously Baby did not desire it—but she did preserve the letter for the rest of her life.

Another admirer, signing himself "Leadville, Col., Aug. 27, 1880. A Friend," being of a more poetic nature, sent her the following verse:

To L. B. D.
Like the morning sun in Summer
Gilding bright the ocean wide,
Like the gentle rain, in summer
Cooling green, the mountain's side,
So your presence here among us,
Fills our hearts with sweet delight.

This must have pleased her ego, for likewise she did not throw it away.

In Leadville there were dozens of gambling places, the most notorious being Pop Wyman's. As respectable women could not be seen in such places, Baby Doe spent many lonely evenings while her lover was engaged with his cards. One night, feeling bored, she decided to buy her favorite oyster supper at the Saddle Rock Café, just a block away from Bill Bush's Clarendon and the Tabor Opera House. She had hardly placed the order when in walked Bill Bush and the Silver King of Colorado, H.A.W. Tabor.

Baby Doe had good reason to remember Bush from her Central City days when, after she had worked at the mine, he had thought her "unladylike" company unworthy to be shared with his precious daughter Antoinette. As for Tabor, she had seen his tall, lanky figure many times on the street. Unconsciously now she found herself studying his face, the dark hair turning gray at the temples; the large friendly eyes, and the hands he always seemed to keep in his pockets.

She thought, "That man is lonely," and felt sorry for him. And then the Silver King seemed conscious of her presence. Their eyes met, and as he turned to address Bush, Baby Doe blushed, for with true feminine intuition she knew the question concerned her. What a good time Bill Bush would have, she thought ruefully, relating the story of her "doubtful past."

Tabor listened intently before speaking. Bush shrugged his shoulders, then called the waiter for a pencil. A few moments later the Miners' Sweetheart was reading a message written informally on the back of a theater program: "Won't you join us at our table?"

It was signed "William H. Bush."

Baby Doe put down the program and gazed once more over to where Tabor sat waiting; then, as if mesmerized by his personality, she walked unsteadily towards him. It was as if instinctively she knew "no later

light would ever lighten up her heaven . . ." For the
next fifty-five years all the Jakes and Harveys of this
world were to be forgotten in her passion for this man
of forty-nine, so many years her senior.

"Leadville the Lusty," the town that never slept — a view of Chestnut Street in the 1870's.

Gold panning in Colorado. Some became bonanza kings. Augusta Tabor's bosom was the first bank in the state.

William H. Bush, cupid, nemesis and sometime friend.

Jesse James, a quiet sojourner in Leadville.

Augusta Louise Tabor, the "First Lady of Leadville."

Baby, the Belle of Oshkosh, as Mrs. Harvey Doe.

Baby Doe Tabor (Copy of a painting by C. Waldo Love). She had a fondness for calla lilies.

H. A. W. Tabor (Juan Menchaca copy of an original painting). His women were loyal, each in her fashion.

Chapter Five

The Veiled Lady

FROM that very evening H.A.W. Tabor and Baby Doe found that they had much in common: a lust for living; a love of showmanship; an interest in mining; a respect for those great Colorado mountains in whose shadow they had made their adopted home.

Baby hated to hurt Jake, for he had always been kind to her. How would he react to her new-found friendship with Tabor? If she was worried, Tabor was not. He had more money now than he knew what to do with; he was a bonanza king—the richest bonanza and carbonate king of them all. What he wanted he had. Besides, Jake Sands was not only a sensible busi-nessman; he was also Tabor's tenant. Jake was offered $5,000 to soothe his hurt feelings, but to his credit he refused to accept it. Gambling man though he was, Jake Sands, like Harvey, really loved Baby Doe.

Then Baby honestly took matters into her own hands. Informing Jake that she had fallen in love with Tabor, she presented him with a diamond ring as a token of her friendship. Jake believed her feelings for Tabor to be true, for he not only accepted the ring but remained on amicable terms with both of them. Years later when he had fallen upon hard times Jake gave the same ring to Sidney Janovitz of Leadville as surety for a $250 loan, soon pleading for its return although he did not have the necessary cash.

"I am very sentimental about that ring. It brings me luck. I promise to make good the loan," he told Jano-vitz, who generously returned it. About a year later Jake gave him some Arizona mining stock to repay the loan, but unfortunately for the accommodating Jano-vitz, the stock proved to be worthless.

If Baby Doe was flattered by the multimillionaire Tabor's attention, she was also apprehensive, as the fol-lowing poem reveals in her scrapbook:

Stolen Love
Oh sweetest is the stolen love,
The apples shaken from the bough
Unseen, unseen, though eyes are keen,
And such a love was ours but now . . .

Underneath she stuck three words clipped from a news-paper: LIZZIE WAS FRIGHTENED.

Despite her own precarious position she saw nothing unusual in scrawling the words BAD WOMAN across a note written by an anonymous woman to Tabor asking him to meet her on a certain street corner.

"Lizzie" had cause to be frightened, for in addition to their "stolen love" she feared that something un-pleasant might happen to Tabor at the hands of those same miners who had once been his friends. The angry men had demanded a minimum wage of $4 a shift, together with an eight-hour working day, absentee ownership and overcapitalization having sown seeds of dissension.

Managers for the Eastern companies refused the de-mands of the miners, most of whom had first come to Leadville seeking overnight riches, only to find the silver-producing area owned by capitalists like Tabor or absentee owner Marshall Field. Faced with starva-tion, the men had to become common miners, for the millionaires had shut the late-comers out. Dishonest Eastern businessmen, who played the New York stock market instead of working the mines themselves, sought by foul means to depress the value of silver stock and then buy it up in order to reap rich profits at a later date.

Mysterious fires broke out in Tabor's Chrysolite Mine, which resulted in the calling out of the fancily dressed Tabor Hose No. 1, complete with their nickel-plated fire engine. When incendiaries failed to get the results they wanted, the grievance-haunted miners became the scapegoats. Hod, once their "Good Old Tabor" because of his frequent kindness in grub-staking them, now found himself cursed by the men he had once helped. Hurt and bewildered, he told Baby Doe, "That's one thing I never have been—mean and stingy." Besides, he loved Leadville, the Cloud City; to him it would always be home.

However, Tabor was worried, for if he was going to run for Governor in the next election, as he planned, he would need the miners' votes.

Together with the other mine owners, he organized a Committee of Safety that met like a secret society in the splendid private rooms in his opera house. Taking as their model the Vigilance Committee of San Francisco, they elected as their chairman C.C. Davis, editor of the *Chronicle*, who approached Governor Pitkin as to the advisability of proclaiming martial law. The governor said that such a course should only be taken as a last resort.

In June 1880, after some lively meetings, marches and ordinary catcalling, martial law was at last imposed, the Tabor Light Cavalry together with other units helping to settle the strike. Tabor had even given a military address from the balcony of the opera house, his remarks being greeted by an ominous silence.

Back in Denver, in spite of her grand White House carriage, Augusta liked to eat in the kitchen because it was near her precious stove. She still liked to bottle fruit and make her own preserves. Among the trees on her splendid new lawn she kept tethered a favorite cow, which she herself milked.

She heard all about her husband's speechmaking during the strike and when he called to see her upon one of his Denver trips, outspokenly expressed her disapproval of his "making a fool of himself." With his ambitions of becoming the next Governor of Colorado he would now need to recultivate the friendships of the miners he had opposed. This was one time that Augusta's views could not upset him, for, as he told her, "It is surprising what political plums money can buy!"

Augusta had heard all about Baby Doe and so had Maxcy, although he was too loyal to mention the fact to his mother. Women friends in Leadville kept her well informed about the mysterious, veiled lady at the Clarendon. She grimly shrugged her shoulders when somebody wrote that her husband was "chivalrously befriending a young widow in weeds." Young widow, indeed! Augusta was still smarting from the memories of the talkative Willie Deville.

When Baby Doe was set up in a newly furnished suite with splendid gold chairs at the Denver Windsor Hotel, of which Tabor was part owner, Augusta was somewhat relieved, thinking that, as in the case of his other paramours, the couple were now close enough to be dealt with. Not for one moment did she believe that Tabor was really in love with the beautiful blonde divorcée. "There's no fool like an old fool," she might

tell her friends, although it riled her to think of all
that good Tabor money being wasted. Three hundred
and fifty dollars' worth of lace and embroidered che-
mises the silly old goat had bought Mrs. Doe from a
traveling peddler. All Leadville, thought Augusta, must
be laughing behind his back!

Baby Doe, still veiled, traveled to Denver by the
new Rio Grande Railway while Tabor took first the
stagecoach to South Park, and then the rival Denver
& South Park Railroad, enjoying the luxury of David
Moffat's private car. The Windsor Hotel boasted just
the kind of high living and elegance that Baby had
always craved. It was much more exciting than the old
American House where she had honeymooned with
Harvey. She was determined that this time her dreams
of grandeur should not be shattered. She had no real
scruples over her "friendship" with H.A.W. Tabor. In
her opinion there was no marriage to break up, hers
already having terminated in divorce, while his had
been on the rocks long before they had ever met.

The Windsor, built with British capital, proudly
boasted of being "the most fabulous hotel in the West."
Rendezvous of all the cattle and bonanza kings, its
grand lobby was regally fitted with heavy red carpet-
ing; red, plush-covered furnishings and mirrors backed
with diamond dust. Fantastic Russian and Turkish baths
boasted Oriental ablutionary parlors all "elegantly fitted
up and handsomely furnished throughout in white
marble." The mahogany bar was sixty feet long, and

advertising announcements described the "Ladies Ordinary" as being particularly "charming."

Tabor placed Maxcy and Bill Bush in charge. In
spite of sixteen years' difference in ages, the newly-
appointed hotel managers were always to remain firm
friends. Tabor, Augusta and Baby Doe all had their
ups-and-downs with Bush, but nothing ever shook
Maxcy's loyal affection for him.

As a young man Maxcy was the most diplomatic son
any couple with marital difficulties could hope to have.
He was devoted to his mother, yet looked after the
very hotel where his father's latest mistress had been
"properly" installed. It was common sense for a fellow
to keep in with so rich a father. In any case, thrifty
Augusta would not have had it any other way, for she
would always fight for her only son's rights.

Maxcy heard with pride that his father planned to
build a hotel of his very own, "such a one as Denver
never heard or even dreamed of." His Tabor Block on
Larimer Street was another project, with the words
Dies faustus chiseled over the archway. It looked like
a mixture of Solomon's temple and a Moslem mosque,
being described at the time as "something new in Colorado architecture." Even strong Colorado granite was
not good enough for this creation; instead, Baby's Crœ-
sus saw fit to transport special stone all the way from
Ohio to build it. The sidewalks were paved to match
the masterpiece.

Tabor now really believed that money could buy

anything, including a marriage to Baby Doe, although he was to find it a costly business before he could finally make her the second Mrs. Tabor. Back in the fall of 1880 Tabor had given Augusta $100,000 as a "parting gift" to ease his conscience, but the first Mrs. Tabor was still very much in the picture. In order to further his political aspirations he even entertained at Augusta's fine mansion. Unfortunately, his discarded wife realized his motives, often shaming him by inviting the servants in to enjoy the musicales with her husband's guests.

Patiently, Baby Doe would sit on her gold chair at the Windsor, waiting for Tabor's return at the end of the meeting. No doubt she spent such interim periods making her scrapbooks. At this period of her life she was very much interested in beauty hints. Among them is the following clipping:

> There is a woman doctor in the town who is waging the most successful warfare against that ofttimes deplorable blemish to beauty, the feminine mustache. . . . Her dimpled arms are otherwise perfect, but their ivory whiteness is marred by black hairs that show so dreadfully when bathing in a sleeveless costume . . .

Thinking that her husband's fling with Baby Doe had continued long enough, Augusta at last decided to take drastic action. In December, 1880, to Tabor's

annoyance, she bought from Charles L. Hall of Leadville a third interest in the Windsor Hotel. With much
pleasure Tabor could have strung up his wife and Hall
together! As part owner, Augusta had no difficulty in
keeping close tabs on the activities of her new acqui-
sition. From her observation post behind a potted palm
she must on various occasions have seen Baby Doe,
still veiled, pass through the lobby. She could not only
check up on her wandering husband but at the same
time draw an excellent monthly dividend from her
"most necessary" investment.

Tabor called her "a damned nuisance," for she
seemed to spend more time at the Windsor than in
her own home, even bringing along her embroidery.
Maxcy, seeking to please both parents, was caught in
the middle of their quarrels. He too had hoped that
Baby Doe would prove only a passing fancy. Instead,
Maxcy was forced to admit that his father had been
leading a much quieter "home" life in his hotel than
he had for the past two years. When Bill Bush, acting
secretly for Tabor, offered to buy out Augusta, she
refused to consider the offer. Even if she had to camp
in front of Baby Doe's suite she was determined to
"shame" Hod back to his senses.

Unfortunately for Augusta, she was dealing with an
equally stubborn and determined woman. Baby Doe
did not leave the Windsor, where she was staying as
a perfectly legitimate guest, even if Tabor was paying
her bills. Exasperated Augusta decided to take a trip

to Europe "to improve her social graces." Surely, she told herself, upon her return Hod would by that time have tired of Baby Doe and would gladly return to her side. If he was determined to pursue his political ambitions, his wife would need to be a good hostess—and she, Augusta Louise Tabor, would stand ready to fill the role. For once she believed this would be money well spent. Unfortunately when Augusta, traveled and "polished," eventually arrived back in Colorado, she found to her chagrin that her rival was still very much in the picture. In fact, all Denver was talking.

Denver, now "Queen of the Plains," was developing a society all its own. The rules of etiquette were strict; the moral reformers strong. Augusta felt that public sympathy would be with her. Even the men were strict when it was a matter of other men's immoralities.

An organization calling itself the Denver Citizens' Protective Association was actually formed to stop waist-conscious "ladies from killing themselves with tight lacing." That old-time gun fighter, Bat Masterson, now owner of a great gambling saloon and variety hall, was formidably opposed by Dean Hart of St. John's Cathedral. Three men—Tom Bowen, Edward Wolcott and H.A.W. Tabor—all destined for senatorship, were almost nightly visitors to Masterson's den of iniquity. The mysterious veiled lady at the Windsor (whose identity everybody knew anyhow) never seems to have scolded him for his nocturnal outings. Besides, she had given him the encouragement he needed to satisfy his dream of erecting in Denver the finest opera building west of the Mississippi, the Tabor Grand Opera House.

Day after day in the privacy of her suite they would go over the exciting plans together. When Tabor's imagination played with the seemingly impossible, Baby Doe never laughed at him as Augusta would have done. She tactfully made her own suggestions, yet took care always to make him feel they were his own. Neither was she ever too tired to listen—not that this was really any hardship on her part, because for the first time in her life she felt a real sense of fulfillment. The difference in their ages never bothered her at all. This was the man she had really been waiting for— the sort of man who built empires. She firmly believed herself destined to share his silver throne.

Eugene Field, Editor of the *Denver Tribune*, who had often poked fun at Tabor, this time had a word of praise, even if it was in verse:

> *The opera house—a union grand*
> *Of capital and labor,*
> *Long will the stately structure stand*
> *A monument to Tabor.*

Edbrooke and Burnham, his architects, their pockets full of Tabor's $1,000 notes, had been dispatched to Europe in search of ideas upon which they were ordered to improve.

A great deal of the real Tabor went into his "modi-

fied Egyptian Moresque" opera house, at its opening
to be described as one of the best in the world. How
Baby Doe loved crimson! Marshall Field supplied
$20,000 worth of upholstery, carpets and furnishings
in this prevalent color. Even the parquet carpet was
a crimson Wilton with relieving border of green.

The theatre—designed, so Tabor maintained, "upon
the selected features of the Covent Garden Theatre,
London, and the Academy of Music, Paris"—combined
the beauty and excellence of both. Multicolored marble
for the lintels, wainscoting and pilasters was shipped
from Italy; heavy silk Louis XIV tapestries costing $50
a yard and boasting Fontainebleau designs came from
France to back the lower boxes and chairs. The repro-
ductions of Italian tapestries that decorated the upper
boxes sported love motifs which delighted the roman-
tically inclined Baby Doe. From the beamed ceiling
hung a gorgeous cut-glass chandelier boasting fifteen
hundred pendants. Over the massive proscenium arch
was a mural of Hector comforting the battle-destined
Andromache.

The stage was splendidly equipped—and how Baby
loved it as she stood there one late afternoon holding
H.A.W. Tabor's hand. The workmen were used to seeing "that hussy in the veil," as more circumspect Den-
verites were calling her. There was an excellent Green
Room and sizable dressing rooms for the stars themselves. Nothing had been overlooked. As for the curtain, it had cost Tabor a small fortune, having been

[108]

painted by Robert Hopkin of Detroit, described as "essentially an artist in temperament," who worked on a movable bridge using "only top quality linen and the best of paints." He covered 720 feet in four weeks, his subject matter being an eerie Roman city falling into decay, a strange choice for a new enterprise.

The opening was set for September 5, 1881. For several days before, editorials in the Denver *News* and the *Tribune* thrashed out the all-important question of whether it would be a "full-dress swallow-tail affair" or not. A letter to the *News* Society editor, signed "Inquirer" and dated August 29, emphasized that "the house is for the city and not for a select few."

An editorial followed, which read in part:

> *Certainly if one wishes and is able to appear in elegant style, there is nothing to be said against it; indeed fair women in exquisite toilets will add greatly to the scene, but let no one who desires to attend the opera and is able to pay the price of admission be kept away on account of the lack of elegant and expensive clothes. The opera house, as "Inquirer" says, "was not built for the select few" but for the people.*
>
> *As for those young men whose incomes would warrant private boxes, full evening toilets and expensive suppers, but whose good taste and good judgment would stand in the way of their going the whole figure, it is hardly necessary to say that it is just such young men Colorado stands in need of. Young men who have brains enough to deport themselves as*

young men, and not as millionaires. They are not only doing what is right and sensible, but they are setting a good example to that class of young men who, at the sacrifice of everything—even honor—will "keep up appearances." Let Denver's young men who are desirous of doing the correct thing in going to the opera, look at the man who owns the magnificent structure as he passes up and down our streets, in attire as plain as that he used to wear before he "struck it rich," before grand, stately edifices bore his name, and let them copy, in this respect, Colorado's plain and unassuming son, whose wealth is fabulous.

It is a false way of living, a seeming to be what we are not, that is costing America so dear.

The reference to the plain attire of the man who "struck it rich" is interesting, for Tabor was always most at home wearing his large black stovepipe hat. On this occasion he seems to have sided with the opposite camp (perhaps on Baby Doe's advice), for he insisted that those attending the grand opening of his Opera House should be "properly dressed."

Once more Eugene Field upheld him, replying to criticism that Tabor's edict "does not furnish good grounds for an assault. The wearing of a dress coat has never been regarded as a crime, even in Colorado. A man who will not wear a dress coat on a dress occasion is a snob . . . When Tabor is before the public as a politician, he is a legitimate subject for criticism.

When he is before it as an enterprising citizen, he is not."

Bill Bush was appointed manager of the new opera house, with the position of treasurer designated to Maxcy, his bosom friend. Maxcy was now courting Luella Babcock, a most respectable young woman, and both Tabor and Augusta wholeheartedly approved of the match. Among the list of boxes for the opening night printed in the *News,* "N.M. Tabor" was allotted his own. The child whose first pants were made from empty flour sacks had now grown up into one of Denver's most eligible bachelors. Although by this time Tabor had told Baby Doe he intended to divorce Augusta, she wondered sometimes if his affection for his only son might prevent his taking the final step.

The Tabor box proper was lettered "A," and as if this were not enough, Baby Doe had suggested a large silver plate, two feet long, to hang on the front, inscribed with the word TABOR. The silver had come from the Matchless.

Meanwhile, in her elegant mansion, the rejected Augusta spent some of her time, like her younger rival, in making up scrapbooks. Augusta's "scrapbooks of trouble," as she called them, were smaller than Baby Doe's and she never wasted a bit of the page. One of them, now in the Western History Department at the Denver Public Library, appropriately had for its cover picture a bird in a silver cage. With her pince-nez spectacles on her long thin nose, Augusta read every item about the new Tabor Grand Opera House that represented the zenith of her estranged husband's career.

Even Dr. Jeffery, eloquent pastor at the First Baptist Church, in his sermon entitled "Worldliness," had seen fit to praise Hod's latest triumph. "Governor Tabor deserves not only individual thanks, but a general and universal tribute from the great public at large, both of Denver and of Colorado," he said, adding that "true religion has no war to make against art or any form of beauty." Augusta quite agreed with him if such "forms of beauty" did not include women like Mrs. Doe. Dr. Jeffery concluded by saying that he hoped the time would come soon when he might himself go to such performances as were to be given at the Denver Opera House; he could see nothing wrong in such attendance—strong words for a nineteenth-century clergyman! Although the building did look more like a Moslem mosque than anything Christian, he further declared that "the building itself, and the operatic performances, were all in harmony with what was good and true and beautiful."

Even the *New York Herald* ran a paragraph on Tabor's triumph, noting that it had cost half a million dollars to build. "The company is composed of sixty-eight people in all and, it is said, they are guaranteed railway fares and $20,000 for the two weeks' engagement."

As she clipped the piece, Augusta was suitably impressed. This would be the Emma Abbott Grand Opera Company. Suddenly Augusta was overcome with a sense of deep hollowness inside. Perhaps she had been too outspoken with Hod; but surely he would ask his legal wife to take her rightful place beside him in Box "A" on opening night, just as she had proudly done in that lonely ox-wagon crossing the open prairie a quarter of a century before!

All these months she had refused to have any communication with him, unless he came home for good; and he (probably thinking the $100,000 parting gift was enough) had not sent her one extra cent for support. Putting down her scissors, on the spur of the moment she decided to write him a letter saying that she was truly sorry for what she had "said in the heat of passion." Would he not allow her to take her proper place with him at the gala opening? Augusta, always a sensitive, well-read woman, thought of all the extra graces she had acquired in Europe. Every well-bred woman in Denver respected her; then how could he so wantonly put her aside?

The begging letter was found among Baby Doe's private papers when she died.

If the Denver gentlemen were finding it difficult to decide what to wear for so auspicious an occasion, the ladies were not. Only the finest silks, satins and velvets were good enough for them. In search of finery, they drove out from their expensive new houses, no two of which seemed alike, for, as it was noted at the time, "The distinguished charm of Denver architecture is its endless variety." Never had the stores specializing in ladies' finery experienced such business, and never had the dressmakers been so overworked. The carriages would stop in front of the stores while their feminine occupants sat comfortably waiting for the materials to be brought outside in order to make their choice.

When the great opening night arrived at last, a ripple of excitement passed through the entire city. Huge crowds gathered in front of the theatre to see the notables arrive. In spite of a slight drizzle the crowd was in a good humor. Across the sidewalk and leading up the steps into the lobby lay a luxuriant red plush carpet. There was a refreshment bar for the men. The theatre proper was gaily decorated with every sort of flower imaginable. Large floral pieces had been made to form the Tabor name. Even the programs, printed on white satin, were unusually extravagant in an era noted for such exotic theatrical items.

Finally an extra-loud cheer rose from the waiting crowd, announcing the arrival of the man of the hour. The curtain rose and Bill Bush, his face wreathed in smiles, proudly came forward to announce the first part of the program. Miss Emma Abbott, he said, unconsciously wiping the tiny drops of perspiration from his forehead, would delight the audience by singing the mad scene from *Lucia*. It was a good choice, for again and again she was recalled to the stage. Amid a great ovation Miss Abbott received a floral harp from Tabor.

Then Lieutenant-Governor Tabor, shuffling, nervous and twisting one end of his long mustache with a thumb and finger, took the center of the stage, having been introduced by "a suitably clad gentleman," who made rather too long a speech in Tabor's honor and presented him with an elaborate gold watch fob as a gift of appreciation from fellow Denver citizens. For a moment Tabor looked somewhat bewildered; then realization of the symbolic significance of the gift came over him. Like a child's, his face beamed with pleasure. Today this fob rests in the Colorado State Museum, Denver. Engraved with pictures of the new Opera House, the Tabor Block, Denver, and the old Tabor grocery store at Oro, near Leadville, the fob also consists of a miniature mine bucket filled with gold and silver nuggets, suspended from a pick and shovel grille. The inscription reads: *Labor omnia vincit.*

Sentimental Tabor! He was so emotionally overcome with both the gift and the deafening applause that he could only choke out a few words of thanks.

Afterwards "honest little Emma," as adoring fans called her, ably supported by her hard-working company, appropriately dedicated the new opera house with three acts of *Maritana.*

Baby Doe, well pleased that she had persuaded Tabor to replace Shakespeare's portrait in the vestibule with his own likeness because "*you* are Denver's benefactor," sat supposedly unrecognized in her veil on the main floor of the theatre, where she could see everything that was going on. Time and again her eyes strayed up to Box H where Maxcy and Luella sat holding hands. Right to the last moment she nervously wondered if, like a queen, Augusta would sweep into Box A, the Tabor family box, to demand her rightful place. As the lights dimmed for the performance to begin she noted with relief that the box was still empty. Tabor was somewhere in the wings; a large pendant of red roses hung somewhat self-consciously over the seats that he and Augusta should rightly be occupying. Of all the society women in Denver, only Mrs. H.A.W. Tabor had stayed away. How the tongues chattered after the performance. . . .

Next evening another large audience attended the Opera House, although this time fewer gentlemen were in formal evening wear. At the end of Emma Abbott's two-week engagement Tabor himself presented her with a star of tuberoses and mixed geraniums. Among her many floral offerings she also received one from a certain Mrs. Doe. Made by Braun & Satterthwaite, the florists, it was in the shape of a star five feet high, with the word ABBOTT picked out in white carnations at its base. One of the Denver papers, conscious of the gossip about Tabor and the Miners' Sweetheart, recorded the fact on September 12. It was Baby Doe's formal introduction to a lifetime of headlines.

Chapter Six

The Story of a Divorce

"No, no, no. 'Those whom God hath joined together let no man put asunder.' "

Augusta Tabor sat rigidly in her straight-backed bottle-green chair facing a slightly bewildered Bill Bush. He had never known such a woman. Here Tabor was offering her practically the earth and yet she still said No to a divorce. Bush, shrewd businessman that he was, had up to that moment believed that anything could be bought. Now he knew that the exception was Augusta Tabor.

Coldly he faced her across the aspidistras. This unpleasant task of acting as emissary in H.A.W. Tabor's domestic affairs was not to his taste. Besides, he didn't like Mrs. Doe—and wasn't Maxcy Tabor, Augusta's son, his best friend? As Bush rose to go he quietly informed Augusta that her husband had no intention whatsoever of visiting her or giving her means of support until she agreed to divorce him. In addition, he was sick and tired of her "keyhole-snooping" at the Windsor Hotel. When she decided to relinquish that investment he, William Bush, would personally buy it.

Tabor was furious when Bush reported the outcome of his futile visit to Augusta. He would give her nothing, he declared; then perhaps she would come to her senses. Neither was he discreet when he spoke of his wife to outsiders, contemptuously referring to her as "the other woman" or "the Broadway woman." Baby Doe was getting restless, egged on by her parents, who were far from happy over her precarious position as Tabor's mistress. Peter McCourt Senior, her father, was a particularly religious man. He could not help but recall how his beautiful daughter had left Oshkosh with such glowing hopes for the future as young Harvey Doe's bride. Now she was divorced and in love with a man old enough to be her father who was not even in a position to "make an honest woman of her."

Mr. and Mrs. McCourt believed Baby when she said that Tabor's marriage had failed before ever he set eyes upon her, yet this did not alleviate her present predicament. They counseled her by letter to prevail upon

Tabor to free himself immediately if he really intended to marry her. Secretly, Mrs. McCourt wondered what Mama Doe would think if Baby were to wed the Silver King of Colorado. Hadn't she once considered her not good enough for "precious Harvey"?

Meanwhile, at her own suggestion, Baby moved to the American House. Denver was gossiping more than ever, so that even if she had worn seven veils it would not have made any difference. Her identity was on everybody's lips, some people insisting she had once been a dance-hall girl. Augusta's faithful women friends carried lurid tales of the goings on at the American House to the "hurt" Mrs. Tabor. They assured Augusta that not only was Baby Doe "a promiscuous hussy" but, worst of all, she used cosmetics. In plain language, "she painted."

Augusta was ready by now to believe anything of her rival, putting her in exactly the same category as the blackmailing Willie Deville and the Indian club swinger. This one, she assured her friends, was "only after the old man's money." Two years earlier Augusta would have berated anybody who dared to call her Hod an "old man"; nor would she have clipped any derogatory pieces about him from the newspapers. Now all was changed; the War of the Tabors had really begun.

Baby Doe seems to have remained the calmest of the three participants in the silver triangle, for she was still hopelessly in love. Since she was unable to appear publicly with her lover, her most usual pastime at the American House still seems to have been making her scrapbooks. When she became depressed, it was her rather impish Irish humor that quickly restored her spirits. Like a naughty child she pasted a calling card bearing the name of her rival MRS. AUGUSTA L. TABOR onto one of the pages, then directly beneath placed a notice advertising the best quality champagne, together with James McEvoy's daring poem:

> With his dark eyelash and
> His purse full of cash,
> His white shining teeth, and his
> Nobby mustache,
> He breaks all their hearts when
> He goes on the mash,
> And I'm the boss girl with
> Charley.

While Baby Doe was thus engaged at her new suite in the American House, and Tabor was dabbling in politics, Augusta put on a cast-iron front that was the admiration of every well-bred female in the city of Denver. In spite of the $100,000 worth of government bonds at four per cent given her by Tabor, she boarded women schoolteachers and others operating in similar respectable capacities. Having been deserted by her husband and left with no visible means of support, she insisted, "I have to do something." If the ladies were shocked, their husbands were amused, for the one thing that Tabor hated was to be called stingy.

Augusta still milked Emily, her cow, on the front lawn where every curious passerby (and there were many) could see her. In summer she grew outsize stalks of Indian corn and for protection bought herself a large hunting dog named Henry Ward Beecher, because she so admired his sister, Harriet Beecher Stowe, who had written *Uncle Tom's Cabin*. Bill Bush, who was now sent almost daily to "wear that woman down" with demands for a divorce, took a dim view of the new addition, who plainly did not like him. And all through his interviews with hawklike Augusta he was forced to keep one eye on her bad-tempered dog. More than once he wished that Baby Doe had never left Central City. Meanwhile, in spite of his domestic difficulties, Tabor's theatrical activities continued to bring culture to Denver and Leadville. Of his many enterprises, with the exception of Baby Doe, Tabor loved best these theatrical ventures. Although his own education had been limited to the little day school at Holland, Vermont, and he did not care for Shakespeare, there were other, lesser, dramatists that he liked.

A showman and an exhibitionist in the Barnum tradition, Tabor was never happier than when surrounded by a merry, jostling crowd. He spent $800,000 upon his Grand Opera House alone. Early in the spring of 1882 it was announced that the great Oscar Wilde would be arriving from England. Eugene Field went so far as to plead that he should be received courteously, "if not as a lecturer, then as one who may yet rank among the strong English poets, for his first volume certainly holds out such hope."

Wilde's Denver lectures were received with mixed emotions for he "never stirred his audience but in the direction of the door." Later many distinguished callers visited his suite at the Windsor, including Tabor, who outdid them all by inviting the aesthete to visit his fabulous Matchless Mine at Leadville. Wilde was thrilled at the prospect, insisting that it was one of his great ambitions to visit a silver mine.

During a spring blizzard in April, 1882, he arrived by rail in Leadville. There was no committee of welcome when, according to local news reports, he went "quietly into the Clarendon Hotel by the ladies' entrance." The high altitude immediately affected his legs; so, dressed in tweeds and "minus either sunflower or lily," he stretched himself full length upon a plush-covered couch and received visitors. One of these described him as being "some six feet tall, with long hair reaching to his shoulders, with a languid far-away look in his eyes, and a mouth vying with Soldene's in size."

Later, in spite of a cold in his stomach, Wilde appeared on the stage of the Tabor Opera House next door, where he was received with more courtesy than he often found upon similar occasions in the East. The *Democrat* remarked, "Whatever may be the value of Wilde's peculiar views, it is certain that he is a gentleman, and as such entitled to ordinary courtesy." Responding favorably, Leadville's citizens spared Wilde the insults of "clever" wags that he had encountered in other, so-called "more intellectual," parts of the U.S.A.

Wilde's lecture was entitled "The Practical Application of the Aesthetic Theory to Exterior and Interior House Decoration, with Observations on Dress and Personal Ornament." Most of his mining audience came more out of curiosity to see the speaker, whose reputation had preceded him, than for any real interest in practical aesthetics. With tongue in cheek Bush had erected a balcony scene upon the large stage, "prettily adorned with bric-à-brac."

Wilde, who is said by a contemporary to have "stumbled on with a stride more becoming a giant backwoodsman than an aesthete" wore a black velvet suit comprising an astounding circular-style cutaway coat, knee breeches, black stockings and buckled shoes. Wearing a "Byron collar with a flossy white neckhandkerchief" and a single cluster of diamonds at his shirt-front, he was described by one contemporary as looking like an "eccentric bishop at a court levee."

"His hair was very straight and long, falling in a dark mass over his shoulders, and was parted directly at the equator. Without much introduction, he proceeded at once to business, pitching his voice at about middle C and inflecting only when tired nature asserted itself and compelled a rising inflection by a long-drawn breath. There was not a comma or a period in the whole hour, save when he came to a stop to take an unaesthetic drink."

Later, while lecturing in England, Wilde said of his Leadville experiences,

> *I went to the theatre to lecture, and I was informed that just before I went there, two men had been brought on the stage at eight o'clock in the evening, and then and there tried and executed before a crowded audience. . . . They are miners—men working in metals, so I lectured to them on the Ethics of Art. I read them passages from the autobiography of Benvenuto Cellini, and they seemed much delighted.*

Between one and two in the morning Wilde was driven to the Matchless wearing a slouch hat, tight trousers, corduroy coat and flat shoes, which seemed so inappropriate for the purpose of descending a mine that Charles Pishon, the mine superintendent, insisted that the poet wear Tabor's own underground suit specially made of India rubber. Eugene Field wrote that the suit, although "having a certain goneness in the length of the pantaloon legs," fitted Wilde quite well.

Later, in his *Impression of America*, Wilde described his descent into the No. 3 shaft of the Matchless on Fryer Hill as being undertaken "in a rickety bucket in which it was impossible to be graceful. Having got into the heart of the mountain, I had supper, the first course being whisky, the second whisky and the third whisky."

Actually the whisky bottle was passed round until everybody had enjoyed twelve "snorters." Of all the participants, miners included, surprisingly only Wilde retained his sobriety, being cheered by all and "voted a perfect gentleman."

Plagued persistently by Bush to divorce her husband, Augusta at last began to waver. She was fearful that Tabor might devise some scheme to defraud her of what she considered her rightful share of his fortune. Besides, there was Maxcy's future to be thought of should Tabor remarry. Her son, who continued to live in his mother's mansion, certainly did not share his father's enthusiasm for Mrs. Doe. Finally in mid-April, 1882, Augusta filed suit in Denver district court for separate maintenance, declaring Tabor's failure to support her for two years, during which time her only means of livelihood had been "by renting rooms in her place of abode, and by keeping boarders." Colorado seethed with gossip over the feuding Tabors.

Augusta demanded not only the family home but the stout sum of $50,000 a year, declaring this to be half of her faithless husband's income. Although her shrewdness and good business sense had never failed her in the past, the injured Mrs. Tabor saw fit to swear that her separate estate was insufficient to maintain her in a "manner and style commensurate with her rank and station in the community."

Tabor spoke the truth when he replied that only recently he had presented her with $100,000, after which she had immediately purchased a third interest in the Windsor Hotel. From this investment the previous year she had received $14,000 as her share of the returns.

Augusta retaliated by asserting that Tabor left their home in July 1880, and since then for months had tried to bribe her with large sums in return for a divorce. In a bill of complaint she listed his assets as follows:

> $9,500,000, citing a few of them as follows: shares in the First National Bank of Denver, $500,000; Matchless Mine $1,000,000; Henriette, Maid of Erin and Waterloo stocks, $1,000,000; interest in the Tam O'Shanter, $1,000,000; diamonds and jewelry, $100,-000; Tabor Grand Opera House, $800,000; Smuggler, Lead Chief and Denver City mines, $500,000; government bonds, $200,000; home property, Brown's Addition, $100,000.

Tabor was the victor in this round of the fight, when, because of certain deficiencies in the Colorado law, the case could not be prosecuted as drawn. Shortly afterwards, in the summer of 1882, he decided to take matters into his own hands by obtaining a fraudulent divorce from Augusta at Durango, a little town in the southwest of Colorado. She was not even consulted. Owning a mine in the vicinity, he had been able to establish a sort of residence there. His well-lined pockets soon persuaded the clerk of the court to paste together the pages recording the illegal proceedings. There the matter might have rested if, following an election shortly afterwards, the clerk had not been replaced. His curious successor pried the pages free, immediately informing Augusta of what he found.

Following the Durango "divorce," Tabor and Baby Doe hastened to St. Louis by separate trains, where they met by arrangement in the office of Colonel Dyer, an attorney who immediately sent for Justice of the Peace John M. Young. Later, at the courthouse where they took out a marriage license, Tabor bribed the recorder, C. W. Irwin, to withhold the Tabor-Doe license information from the press.

Tabor, happy as a schoolboy who had stolen apples from a forbidden tree, whispered to his bride, "Secretly divorced and secretly married. That'll be something for Augusta to swallow about the man she thinks she can keep tied down! It's also a good precaution for those scandalmongers at the Senate. If they get too nosey, we'll show them we're really married."

Baby Doe was not so optimistic as her "dear Tabor," for she was not the sort of girl who enjoyed getting married in secret. Their taking out a scrap of paper did not, somehow, seem really binding. Brought up a strict Catholic, Baby Doe believed that marriages could be solemnized only in church. That night in their hotel she tried not to reveal her discomforting thoughts to the exuberant "bridegroom."

THE TWO LIVES OF BABY DOE

At five o'clock on the afternoon of January 2, 1883, a reporter from the Denver *Republican* chanced to wander into the County Court Room to stumble upon one of the biggest newspaper scoops in his city's history. There were six people in the large room: Judge Harrington, County Clerk Steele, Sheriff Spangler, Attorney Amos Steck and Attorney Rockwell—*and a woman.*

The reporter's eyes bulged with excitement, for the woman on the stand was none other than Mrs. Augusta Louise Tabor, estranged wife of the Lieutenant-Governor of Colorado. She was plainly dressed in a brown ensemble with small round hat, and her outer coat was open to reveal a simple brooch that only she knew contained a lock of her wandering husband's hair. She nervously fingered the muff that lay in her lap. Mrs. Tabor was seeking a divorce.

So excited was the *Republican* reporter and so cold were his fingers that he found it hard going to get the details into his notebook. His nose was dripping from the remains of a head cold, but he did not have time to wipe it.

As the minutes passed the excited reporter learned that Mrs. Tabor was seeking a separation from her wealthy husband on the solitary ground of desertion. In a quiet, cultured voice she testified that "Mr. Tabor" had deserted her without cause in the summer of 1880, and since the January following that summer, had not contributed one dollar towards her support. When asked by Judge Harrington if there were any collusion between herself and Governor Tabor in trying to procure a divorce, she hesitated for some time before admitting there was. Her attorney, Steck, immediately intervened.

"The collusion," he insisted in a voice that bore the ring of truth, "exists only so far as Mrs. Tabor consented to take a certain sum of money to procure a divorce from the defendant, and in no other respect was there collusion between the parties."

The judge appeared satisfied. He motioned Augusta to continue. Wearily she began to speak, as if she had gone over what she was about to say a thousand times before:

"The Governor has given me the La Veta Place [*an exclusive apartment building*] and the house in which I now live. I value them at $250,000; that is all." Augusta swallowed hard, her voice incredibly sad.

Attorney-for-the-Defense Rockwell then took the stand, while Augusta refused a glass of water offered her by Mr. Steck. Rockwell, a smile on his face, said he was quite willing to admit everything charged in the plea. When asked about Governor Tabor's having secured a divorce at Durango the previous March, he replied without trace of embarrassment that he knew the "divorce" was procured.

This was too much for Augusta. "*Fraudulently!*" she shouted in a loud voice, throwing her muff onto the empty chair beside her. The sole reporter scribbled away at his notes, not daring to pause long enough even to take a good breath.

"Yes, fraudulently," interrupted Steck.

Rockwell shrugged his shoulders, shifting uneasily in his hard chair. His thickening neck had turned quite red.

"I told Mr. Tabor," he admitted at last. "I told Mr. Tabor that it was not worth the paper it was written upon, and advised him to secure another. I have been working for that for some time." The Attorney for the Defense extracted a clean white handkerchief from one of his pockets and dabbed at the little moisture spots that had appeared all over his forehead.

Then, asserting there was nothing more to be said, Steck hoped his Honor would grant the decree.

Suddenly Augusta's tearful voice rang through the empty courtroom. "Judge," she pleaded, with all the pride of a Catherine of Aragon, "I wish you would enter upon the record, 'Not willingly asked for. . . .'" She could say no more for, as the *Republican* reporter ably reported, "Here her feelings so overcame her that she burst into tears, and repeated over and over for all to hear, "O God! not willingly, not willingly!"

Even the Attorney for the Defense was visibly shaken, his face turning deathly white like Augusta's. Momentarily he felt nothing but loathing for Lieutenant-Governor Tabor. Standing there confronting the wronged Augusta, he was conscious of being the unwilling scapegoat for his eminent client's domestic failings.

THE STORY OF A DIVORCE

Summing up later, Judge Harrington said he was satisfied that the plaintiff's story was true in every particular; he had no hesitancy in granting the plea—and, as the reporter noted, "with a few scratches of the pen, Hon. H.A.W. Tabor and Mrs. Augusta L. Tabor were declared legally separated and free to marry again." He continued:

When Mrs. Tabor was handed a paper to sign, she turned to Mr. Steck, and said, with an hysterical sob, "What is my name?"

"Your name is Tabor, ma'am," he replied. "Keep the name; it is yours by right."

"I will," she answered; "it is mine till I die. It was good enough for me to take. It is good enough for me to keep, judge. I ought to thank you for what you have done, but I can not, I am not thankful; but it was the only thing left for me to do," and bowing to the court she left the room, as Mrs. Tabor, but the wife of Governor Tabor no more.

After the court had adjourned, Amos Steck appeared to notice the *Republican* reporter for the first time. The reporter was quietly transcribing his notes when Augusta's attorney bore down upon him like an enraged bull. "It is a pity that thing has to go in the papers. You are nothing but a set of scandalmongers. That's what you are."

The reporter was incensed. In his opinion as a gentleman of the press, a "secret" public hearing was definitely underhand. Without raising his voice he gave the learned attorney a piece of his newspaper mind.

"We know exactly where to get scandal. When we see lawyers hovering around, a corpse of some fair name is not far off."

"That's so," grumbled Steck, feeling now at some disadvantage, and realizing too late that his bad temper might be recorded in the next day's paper; "but that woman has suffered. I know all about it. If the truth were known, it would be enough to ruin Tabor forever. She knows all about it, yet loves the man so that she will not say a word. Oh, she knows all about his practices with lewd women! I never saw such a woman. She is crazy about Tabor. She loves him and that settles it. It is another Napoleon and Josephine case out and out. Tabor has never had any luck since he deserted his wife. It will be a poor day, and then he will go to her and she will help him." That evening the energetic *Republican* sent reporters to interview both H.A.W. and Augusta, and neither of them showed any reluctance to speak their minds. Augusta adored newspapers and still earned herself pin money by sending little dispatches to the Eastern press. The account of both interviews obtained that evening she diligently clipped for her scrapbook.

At nine in the evening the reporter discovered Tabor standing talking politics with another man on the grand staircase leading from the rotunda to the second floor of the Windsor Hotel. When they parted, the reporter asked the lieutenant-governor if he might obtain a statement from him. Tabor readily consented, inviting him upstairs to the suite of rooms looking out upon Eighteenth Street—the same suite so recently vacated by Mrs. Doe.

When Tabor had seated his visitor in a comfortable chair he offered him a cigar and a drink, both of which were gratefully accepted. Finally the reporter said, "I see by the records of the courts today, Governor, that Mrs. Tabor secured a divorce from you. As the matter is one of public record, would you mind telling the *Republican* all the facts connected with the case?"

"Why, certainly not," said Tabor amiably, tugging at one end of his long mustache, a characteristic habit of his. "The matter has been telegraphed by the *Associated Press*, and there is nothing private about it."

He paused for a moment, then continued. "I am a citizen of Colorado and I have extensive interests in La Plata county. A divorce was granted me in that county some time ago. I brought suit for divorce in that country and obtained a decree in my favor."

"Was that divorce considered regular and lawful?" asked the reporter.

"To be sure it was," assured Tabor, taking a sip at his whisky. "I have at least three witnesses by whom it can be proved that the legal papers were served upon Mrs. Tabor." He shrugged his shoulders. "But I do not care to talk about that. Mrs. Tabor objected to some portions of the proceedings at Durango, and she expressed a willingness to bring suit herself in Arapahoe County on the grounds of desertion. The suit was brought on these grounds, and came up today. My lawyers made no objections to the plea, and the case was decided in four hours—the shortest divorce case on record."

The reporter nodded. "And you are satisfied with the termination?" he asked tactfully.

"Perfectly," laughed the governor, as if to put his visitor again at ease. "It has caused me a great deal of worry and trouble for some time, and I may say I feel relieved and happy."

Here the reporter noted that again Tabor smiled "and rubbed his hands together as if he were at peace with himself and the balance of mankind."

"It has cost me some three hundred thousand worth of property," Tabor then volunteered, "but I am satisfied."

"You have given her, in settlement, the homestead in which she now lives and the La Veta Place?" the reporter ventured to confirm."

"Yes."

"At what do you value the property?"

"The homestead is rated at one hundred thousand and La Veta Place at two hundred thousand. The latter property cost one hundred ninety-eight thousand exclusive of the ground." Tabor puffed at his cigar and fingered the precious watch fob given him by the grateful citizens of Denver.

"And what will the rents from La Veta Place amount to monthly?" the reporter persisted.

"From one thousand one hundred to one thousand two hundred."

"This seems like a very liberal settlement," suggested the reporter.

"Yes, but I got off easier than I would if the case had come up in another way. I might have been compelled to make an itemized showing of my property if the case had been brought into court in another form. Then it would have cost me more than one million."

Tabor continued somewhat importantly, "I have interests from Texas to Maine. It would have caused a great deal of trouble and expense to have been compelled to get up such a statement. And she would have been allowed one-fourth of the amount, you know." Here "a pleased expression flitted over the governor's face." For a moment he looked like a mischievous child who has escaped punishment for doing something wrong.

"You gave your wife several thousand dollars in cash a few years ago, did you not?" inquired the interested reporter.

"About three years ago I gave her one hundred thousand in four per cent government bonds."

The reporter carefully noted the figure, then suddenly, as if to catch Tabor off-guard, demanded, "Then you do not care to say anything further about the

Durango divorce case?" His cheeks turned an orange-pink as he waited for the answer.

"There is nothing further to say," insisted Tabor, "except that I know nothing about the report of the two leaves pasted together in the court records at Durango. That is news to me, as much as it has been or will be to anyone."

Up to that point no mention had been made of the pasted leaves. The reporter faithfully made note of what Tabor said, although he did not really believe him. "One more question, Governor," he asked slowly. "You have heard, of course, the report that soon after procuring a divorce at Durango you were married to Mrs. Doe. Is there any truth in this report?"

Tabor had obviously been expecting to be asked this sooner or later. He was also prepared to lie. Coming from his bluff, genial lips his reply sounded hollow indeed. "The person who started that report certainly had very little to do."

"Then I am to understand the report is not true?" asked the reporter.

"There is not a word of truth in it," responded the governor emphatically, but then, as if remembering Baby Doe, he softened his tone considerably. "But that's not saying I wouldn't like to. She's a nice lady," he smilingly admitted.

Just then some political friends arrived to see him, so that the lieutenant-governor was forced to excuse himself. The reporter noted that Tabor had during the entire interview "refrained from saying an unkind word against Mrs. Tabor and avoided touching upon anything that would tend to bring her into unnecessary prominence." The other *Republican* reporter—the one who had been at the actual divorce proceedings— went in search of Augusta and was greeted cordially at her fashionable mansion. He found her sitting in an easy chair, her head bandaged. She was suffering, she said, from a nervous headache.

Explaining his mission, Augusta remarked with some resignation, "You were in the courtroom this afternoon. I recognize you now. I am sorry it has to go in the papers."

The young reporter smiled. He was, Augusta thought, just about her Maxcy's age. She supposed that he had to make a living.

"Would you be willing to make a statement of any kind, Mrs. Tabor?" he asked, somewhat appealingly.

"Oh, no!" she exclaimed, her voice more startled than unkind. "No statement is needed now. Mr. Tabor has secured what he has been working for for years. He is happy, and I am satisfied if he is happy." She compressed her lips, determined not to cry in front of this "boy."

"When did you consent to secure a divorce from Mr. Tabor?"

"Only a few days ago. I knew he would never live with me again, and it was all I could do. You heard me say, however, that the divorce was not secured willingly."

The reporter nodded. "You heard about the

Governor's having secured a divorce at Durango. Did he?"

Augusta swallowed hard. "Yes, he did," she exclaimed, her voice turning shrill. "But it was fraudulent. I will tell you. The first I heard of it was a month or two after it had been procured."

"Go on," prompted the reporter. This was just what he wanted. . . .

"How I came to hear of it at all was owing to the fact that there was a new country clerk in that county, who had as much curiosity as a woman," said Augusta tartly. "When he took possession of his office he found two leaves pasted together in his record book, and by soaking in water and prying with a knife he found out that a bill of divorce had been granted to Governor Tabor. The clerk wrote us about it," she added with satisfaction, "which was the first—and the very first— I had heard about it."

"Were no papers served upon you?" asked the young reporter, trying to look incredulous.

"Upon my honor, no," insisted the injured Augusta. "Why, the most shameful things were alleged against me, and do you suppose I would submit to that? Governor Tabor knows that he could not get a divorce from me in any court in the state, and do it lawfully. I told Governor Tabor so in the State House last summer in Governor Pitkin's room in the presence of his private secretary. Governor Tabor knows, and knows well, that the allegations he made against me at Durango are false."

She had said what she wanted to. Dabbing nervously at her lips with a lace-edged handkerchief, Augusta awaited the next onslaught. "My," she thought, "what a boy he is to be asking me such personal questions."

"Did he perjure himself?" the reporter snapped.

Augusta hesitated just for a moment, remembering a tall, lanky young man and a prairie schooner. She had loved that tall, lanky young man. How could she call him a liar now?

"There are persons in this world who do things they could be sent to the penitentiary for—but they have money," she finally answered. "The idea of convicting of a crime a man worth millions is ludicrous."

"Did he ever tell you why he has treated you the way he has?" The young reporter spoke quietly. This sad, tired-looking woman reminded him of his mother.

"No," said Augusta. "I have never been able to get a word out of him. Oh, I hope he will feel as happy as I feel miserable. He will go to the Senate, I suppose, while I will have to sit here and long and wait for my time to come. It has been the ambition of his life."

Chapter Seven

A Wedding Has Been Arranged

If H.A.W. Tabor had stuck to his business and theatrical enterprises instead of invading the world of politics, his life might have ended differently. His political ambitions proved a great mistake, although he never admitted it. His record as lieutenant-governor was not unsatisfactory; contemporary reports show the former stonecutter competently presiding over the state senate. However, writing in the State Historical Society publication, "The Tabor Story," Edgar C. McMechen asserts:

Tabor would have done well to take warnings from the character of attacks made upon him during his first gubernatorial campaign. These had nothing to do with the later attacks, based upon his marriage with Baby Doe, as he had never heard of her at the time. Colorado was then in the grip of some wily, ruthless politicians. These men had no intention of allowing one whom they regarded as a political inter-loper to usurp what they regarded as their vested interest in the seats of the mighty. In those days anything went in a political campaign. W.A.H. Loveland, builder of the Colorado Central Railroad and a political power, recently had bought the Rocky Mountain News *from W.N. Byers. While not a candidate for office himself he was a supporter of Senator N.P. Hill and his entourage. Tabor did not fit into the Hill schemes. During the summer and fall of 1878, the* News *went the limit.*

Such comments as these about Tabor were common: "a shambling, illiterate boor . . . Mormonism and infidelity go hand in hand on the Republican ticket . . . Tabor's money, largely gleaned from the gulches of Lake County by the aid of Chinese cheap labor . . . If both of Tabor's wives should take the stump . . . what a red hot canvass they would make . . . in case he reached gubernatorial dignity . . . the can-can will be given with modern improvements." Later in the campaign Loveland increased the number of Tabor "wives" to four.

Nevertheless, Tabor was successful, largely because

*he was running on a Republican ticket headed by
Pitkin, and Pitkin was strong with the church element.
Tabor filed a $30,000 slander suit against the* News,
*probably for propaganda purposes, because no one
could collect for slander from a newspaper in those
days.*

After James Abram Garfield was shot July 2, 1881,
by a disappointed office-seeker named Charles J.
Guiteau, the new President, Chester A. Arthur, made
Colorado Senator Henry M. Teller Secretary of the
Interior. This meant that upon the Senate's convening
in January 1883 a vacancy had to be filled by the legislature, in addition to a full, six-year Senate term. Tabor's
friends asked Governor Pitkin to give him the vacancy
until such time as the legislature met, but Pitkin, want-
ing the longer term for himself, had no desire to build
up an opponent. Tabor might have proved a formid-
able rival after presenting the community with such a
civic gift as the Opera House, and selling at a bargain
price the land for Denver's new post office.

Pitkin took less than a week to appoint George M.
Chilcott, a lawyer, "certainly not brilliant but generally
regarded as an eminently respectable politician," to fill
the gap. Pitkin requested Tabor's promise not to run
for the seat at the coming election, but the latter
bluntly refused, instead forming rather a surprising
alliance with a somewhat notorious character, Jerome
Napoleon Chaffee, banker and speculator. Everybody

but Tabor believed that Chaffee coveted for himself
the senator's post, which he had once held. Eugene
Field, amused by the strange union, printed with
relish,

> *Chaffee had a little lamb*
> *Who wore a fierce mustache,*
> *And people wondered how that lamb*
> *On Chaffee made a mash.*

> *What makes this Chaffee love the lamb?*
> *Incessantly they cried.*
> *The lamb has got a golden fleece,*
> *The knowing ones replied.*

Chief candidates in the bitter campaign for the
legislative appointment were Governor Pitkin, Tabor,
ex-Governor J. L. Routt, William A. Hamill and Thomas
M. Bowen of Del Norte—believed to be Tabor's friend
—who had made $3,000,000 in the Little Annie Mine.
After ninety-five ballots Pitkin's supporters concluded
that it was impossible to break the deadlock with Tabor
and suddenly shifted their support to Tom Bowen, "the
coolest poker player in the whole State of Colorado,"
who, on the ninety-seventh ballot, won the longer term.
Tabor, believed to have paid most of the Republicans'
1882 campaign expenses estimated at $200,000, was
offered the smaller, thirty-day term. Although he
realized that he had been made a political football, he
did not complain. His acceptance is evidence of the

best in the contradictory character that was H.A.W. Tabor:

> *You have seen fit to favor me with an election to the short term, the baby term, which it is, being for only thirty days. It is not always that one who goes in for the big prize is put off with one seventy-second part of it, but I have been. Yet I am very thankful, and am satisfied, especially as you have secured a capable gentleman for the long term. As I will be in Washington but thirty days I will be able to be of but little service, but I shall do what I can and shall take special pains to commend the state to the kind consideration of the President. I again, gentlemen, extend my thanks for the honor conferred.*

There were those who heard him who smiled at his naïveness, not realizing that Tabor the Silver King of Colorado had a special reason for desiring a U.S. Senatorship in Washington if only for thirty days. He had promised Baby Doe riches and honors. Why not marry her—for what was really the second time if one counted the St. Louis ceremony—in Washington, with all the pomp and splendor that money could buy? The idea appealed to his sense of showmanship. They could even invite President Arthur to the wedding. What red-blooded American girl could ask anything more splendid than that?

With much fanfare Tabor set out for Washington.

[145]

Today he would have been the joy of every gossip columnist in the country, but even in his own era the press had a field day. Much printed about him was so farfetched as to be ludicrous. According to one report, Tabor, while traveling on the train to Washington, had asked to have his berth made up early, when ". . . a gorgeous velvet cap, elaborately decorated, was first produced and hung on a hook for all to see. Next followed a magnificent ruffled nightshirt, half smothered with costly point lace of the finest quality, which the Senator said was worth $250."

On February 3, 1883, Tabor took his oath of office. He was dressed in black, and his initial accessories incuded a pair of outsize gold cuff links with onyx and diamond settings, and a large diamond solitaire on each hand. When discreetly told by a friendly senator that his brilliants were out of place, Tabor readily discarded them.

Eugene Field's Denver *Tribune* reported that Tabor had introduced a bill for the suspension of gold coinage, and declared that "Tabor, having obtained the floor, kept the whole Senate at bay for three hours, delivering the most powerful address heard in the Senate since the great French Arms debate. He analyzed the bill to the dregs, and was at times ferociously satirical . . ." Actually, the thirty-day Senator from Colorado made no address at all during his short term in office. He did second a solitary motion and he did propose two bills of his own, both of which by present standards appear very feasible. He suggested an appropriation of $100,000 to establish a military post in Colorado (today Colorado Springs is the site of the 17,500-acre U.S. Air Force Academy and headquarters of the North American Air Defense Command, the first two-country all-service military command to operate on the North American continent); and a like sum to preserve the forests of the West.

Simple and downright, Tabor did not deserve the ridicule he received. Eugene Field printed a sarcastic story of Tabor's debut into so-called high society . . .

Tabor spent Sunday in New York as the guest of the Honorable Roscoe Conkling. "Tabor," remarked Conkling to a New York Herald *reporter last evening, "is a charming fellow. He is full of anecdotes and* bon mots, *and quicker at repartee than any man I know. As we sat at table this afternoon, Vanderbilt, who is something of a wag, was inclined to banter Tabor for cracking nuts between his teeth, instead of using the silver implements provided for the purpose. "What has become of your crackers, Horace?" said he. Quick as a flash, Tabor retorted, "I ate them in my soup an hour ago!" Ha, ha, ha! a merry fellow—full of jest and song and mirth when occasion demands.*

To Tabor's credit, he took without retaliation or malice the ribbing he received at the hands of some of the gentlemen of the press. Certainly according to present-day newspaper practice he would have been within his rights to sue for libel. Where he showed lack of judgment and good taste was in planning a lavish wedding for himself and Baby Doe when his official divorce from Augusta had been obtained only a few weeks before. Certainly his love knew no bounds if the ceremony was an indication of the lengths to which he was prepared to go in her behalf.

Meanwhile Baby was in Oshkosh, visiting her parents, who were delighted that their future son-in-law, with a generous gift of $150,000, had recouped their lost fortune. On February 23, 1883, Baby received a letter from her bridegroom-to-be, written in dignified grandeur from the United States Senate:

> *My darling*
> *Everything is working all right. I have quite a* grand *dinner party tomorrow night in fact the best that has been held here for a long time and I do not know that it has ever been excelled. I have to it The President . . .*

The President of the United States! Baby was thrilled. What girl wouldn't be? Her mother made sure that Mama Doe was informed that her ex-daughter-in-law's future husband was important enough to be entertaining presidents. All Oshkosh was agog with the news. The McCourt family were in mourning, for Baby's good-looking brother James, who had married the actress, had recently died after breaking his leg in a freak accident. According to an Oshkosh newspaper, "only a few minutes before he expired he lit a cigar and smoked part of it, saying to his brother, 'They ain't going to bury me, yet awhile, hey Pete?'"

James's death left Baby Doe in a delicate family predicament, for she had allowed him to deposit in his safety-deposit box at the National Bank of Oshkosh the jewelry, valued at $15,000, given her by Jacob Sandelowsky. Tabor might have been jealous that his bride-to-be cared to wear jewels given her by another (and much younger) man. James's creditors promptly seized the jewels and would have kept them if H.A.W. Tabor had not generously put up the necessary bonds pending the suit to determine their real ownership.

Tabor's dinner, held February 24, 1883, at the Willard Hotel, Washington, was given—according to a Washington paper—"to the few people who have been polite to him." This minority included President Chester Alan Arthur, whose attendance tended to refute the claims of Tabor's enemies and detractors a few days later when they maintained that the President had been shamefully deceived and "dragged" to the wedding. The truth was that the President of the United States did not find Senator Tabor repugnant at all.

Besides the Chief Executive, the dinner guests included ten senators, six congressmen, Senator-Elect Bowen of Colorado, and Colonel William H. Bush (relieved, no doubt, that Tabor and Augusta were truly divorced at last). The menu was lavish: Philadelphia

Capon, *à la Godard;* sweetbreads, *à la Conti;* Canvas-back duck; fillet of beef, larded, with mushrooms; omelet; soufflé, and broiled shad, *à la maitre d'hotel.* With so many French words floating around his Washington dinner table the unwelcome thought passed through Tabor's mind that, with her new European "polish," as she called it, Augusta would have felt quite at home there.

When the bride of the year, her delighted parents, two of her brothers, two sisters and their respective husbands reached Washington, the bride diligently addressed the envelopes for the wedding invitations in her own handwriting. The invitations had lush quarter-inch silver margins, and the inscriptions were engraved in silver.

Baby Doe received her first rebuff when none of the wives of the Colorado executives in Washington would come, but perhaps the cruelest insult came from the wife of Judge James Belford, Colorado's only congressman at the time, who sent the invitation, torn in half, straight back to the bride by her coachman.

Mrs. Belford, one of Colorado's most enthusiastic temperance workers, had known of Baby Doe during their Central City days, for her husband, at that time very much in favor of women's suffrage, had greatly admired Baby Doe's initiative when she worked like a man in the Fourth of July.

Later, while writing to a friend in Denver as Secretary of the Interior, Teller thus summed up the wedding invitation problem: "I humiliated myself to attend his wedding because he was Senator from Colorado—but Mrs. Teller would not . . . he made a great fool of himself with reference to that woman, and he ought now to retire and attend to his private affairs."

Although Mrs. Belford and company explained their conduct as loyalty to the first Mrs. Tabor, declaring that Augusta had agreed to divorce Tabor simply to save him from a possible charge of bigamy, the Central City *Register* had an entirely different interpretation—jealousy. A paragraph ran:

Mrs. Doe is well remembered both here and in Blackhawk. She made her home with her husband in Central for quite a period of time, and her plump form and vivacious ways made her the object of great admiration from the masculine sex and a corresponding amount of envy and jealousy on the part of the females. *She was recognized while here as a woman of many strong and worthy qualities. She knew the right and dared to do it. She is at last rewarded by becoming the bride of the richest man in the Silver State.*

Mrs. Teller, when asked by a reporter why she also had refused "with cold regrets" to attend Baby Doe's wedding, exclaimed, "Not for ten thousand dollars. I think it would have been an insult to the real Mrs. Tabor."

At nine o'clock on the evening of March 1, Baby Doe walked proudly down the grand stairway of the Willard Hotel on the arm of her father, for her public marriage to H.A.W. Tabor. She was wearing a white moire wedding gown with a long train and marabou trimmings, a traditional tulle veil with orange blossoms, and white kid gloves that extended above the elbows. The elaborate gown cost $7,000, and Baby's lingerie was made of real lace. Tabor's agents had been sent to Europe to locate the jewels that Queen Isabella of Spain had pawned to make possible Columbus's discovery of America. The agents duly reported success and the gullible Tabor asked for no proof of authenticity when the collection of brilliant gems was delivered to him. Unfortunately, the diamonds— including one specifically known as the Isabella Diamond—could not be assembled in necklace form before the wedding.

The only women present at the ceremony were Baby Doe's McCourt relatives, appropriately dressed in deep mourning for her brother James. Although their gowns were made of the finest silk, Tabor thought they looked "like a group of black crows," so he gave them all expensive diamond, onyx and jet brooches to offset their sinister appearances.

The ceremony was to be performed by the Reverend Placide Louis Chapelle, who later became Archbishop of New Orleans, as the couple stood before an ornately carved table draped with a rich cardinal-red altar cloth. Above it hung a large wedding bell of sweet-smelling white roses held in place by a floral arch. This was surmounted by a heart made of red roses, pierced by an arrow of violets shot from a Cupid's bow of heliotrope. The wedding ring was signified by a circle of red roses lying beneath the bell.

At each end of the table was a large four-leaf clover, placed there both as a good luck symbol and a generous gesture to Baby's Irish parents for providing such a beautiful bride. The candelabrum with ten lighted tapers illuminated the arrangements of Jacqueminot roses, white camellias and violets. A garland of rose-buds and smilax ran round the entire length of the table, and even the pillars of the room were garlanded. Huge potted palms flanked the fireplace with its over-mantel mirror of glittering gold.

As Baby Doe entered the wedding suite her eyes lighted with mingled pleasure and admiration, for the room seemed like fairyland. Fresh violets were strewn in her path as she slowly advanced toward the glimmer-ing bridal bower.

The service was in the form of an abbreviated nuptial mass, at the conclusion of which President Arthur stepped forward "fittingly to congratulate" the happy pair. He then told Baby Doe, "I have never seen a more beautiful bride. May I not beg a rose from your bouquet?" Baby Doe lowered her lovely eyes before complying with the presidential request, then pressed the blossom into his lapel; and the President's side-whiskers "delightfully tickled" her pink cheek as he kissed her. "It's like heaven," her excited mother whispered, loudly enough for all in the room to hear. Tabor, in his fine dress suit with a white velvet waistcoat, was beside himself with happiness and pride.

On "each dish of dainty viands" at the reception following the ceremony were colorful spring posies, and the buckets of champagne were garlanded with "chaste white flowers."

President Arthur spent most of his time talking to the bride and eventually left at ten forty-five. At midnight everything was over.

HORACE A.W. TABOR,
LIZZIE BONDUEL McCOURT,
Married
Thursday, March First
Eighteen Hundred & Eighty-Three
Washington, D.C.

So ran the official announcement cards. The wedding caused a national sensation—especially in Denver, where Augusta's mansion was filled with friends trying to console her. She wept all the next night and, according to her own admission, cried herself to sleep every night for the next ten years. Of all the newspaper stories, true or fictitious, concerning the wedding, none received more sensational publicity than the one describing Tabor's $250 pink silk nuptial nightshirt with insertions of rosepoint lace and solid gold buttons. Although Baby Doe sentimentally saved everything, including her wedding dress, this exotic nightshirt—if it ever did exist—failed to turn up among her possessions at the time of her death. There were, however, several pairs of pajamas, including some made of the finest white French flannel, and Baby's embroidery needle was found in the feather-stitching of an unfinished jacket.

The *Albany Journal* saw fit to print an intimate picture of the bride:

> *Mrs. Tabor is without doubt the handsomest woman in Colorado. She is young, tall, and well proportioned, with a complexion so clear that it reminds one of the rose blush mingling with the pure white lily; a great wealth of light brown hair that is always dressed in a simple but artistic manner and shows that it grew on the head that wears it; large, dreamy blue eyes that sometimes kindle with enthusiasm, twinkle and flash like that brilliant gem that fastens the lace about her swan-like neck; a Mary Anderson mouth and chin, and a shoulder and bust that no Colorado Venus can compare with; delicate feet and a tiny white hand with tapering, white fingers, and I have done with this pen picture, except to add that she is onostentatious [sic]; that she dresses richly, but in good taste, and that when she walks she moves as majestic as a queen. She shows also a sweet disposition and an affectionate and genuine nature.*

In contrast, the Washington Correspondent of the *New York Tribune* blasted forth,

> *A cold shudder has gone through Washington at the rumor that the Colorado man (Senator Tabor) liked Washington, intended to build here and live.*
>
> *There is nothing in Daudet so picturesquely vulgar as this gorgeous hotel wedding of a pair who had been married for months already, but were determined to have the éclat of being married over again in a senatorial capacity . . .*

A more kindly correspondent suggested that "those who try to make it unpleasant for the pretty little woman who married Tabor and whose life had known little of peace and comfort before she met him are people who would like mighty well to step into her little shoes."

Father Chapelle was horrified at the newspaper reports of the wedding, declaring that until that time he had no idea of the divorced status of both bride and groom. He returned the $200 wedding fee given him by Tabor and to this day the marriage is not listed in the parish register of St. Matthew's, Washington. It is amazing, with all the ballyhoo published far and wide concerning the Silver King's divorce from Augusta, that none of the Colorado women living in Washington had, to spite Baby Doe, informed him beforehand.

The good father firmly maintained that he had taken all the necessary precautions as to Tabor and Baby

Doe's marital status before administering the Sacrament of Marriage. The bride's father had "clearly told" him that there was no impediment in the eyes of the church to such a union.

The priest threatened to have the marriage called illegal, in answer to which threat Tabor declared in the press that "Father Chapelle did not ask me or Miss McCourt whether either of us had been divorced or not." He also sent the long-suffering Bill Bush over to see and pacify the priest, which he evidently did, because the matter was dropped. Baby Doe was to spend years as a penitent to expiate what she later believed to be a great sin—the deception of her Church.

The second Mrs. Tabor's short stay in Washington was far from over. On March 5 Washington society was invited to the White House to honor Mary Arthur McElroy (Mrs. John McElroy of Albany, the President's sister) who acted as official hostess of the White House for her brother, a widower since 1880. His only daughter, Ellen, ten years old when he became President, was too young to assume her rightful duties as mistress of the White House.

Mrs. McElroy might have been the instigator of the party but Mrs. H.A.W. Tabor received the most critical attention. A correspondent of the *State Register*, Washington, under the heading WASHINGTON SMALL TALK paints a picture of that memorable day:

There is a crush at the White House today; the

whole city seems to be here for the purpose of paying its respects to Mrs. McElroy, the sister of President Arthur, a small, delicate lady, who stands at the head of a long line of distinguished American women in the Blue Parlor. The Marine Band, under Philip Sousa, greets the visitors with choice selections from different operas, the Pirate's Song in Penzance being the one rendered as we passed the outer door of the vestibule. The new opalescent glass doors of the corridor looked very beautiful under the gas jets, as if they were crystal and pearl. Andrews' picture of the late General Garfield hangs in the corridor, midway between the Conservatory and the East room, arresting the attention of visitors by its faithful likeness and careful handling. In the recess of the walls are rare and costly plants, blooming in gilt wicker baskets to all appearance, but really they are concealing the pots where the flowers draw their life. Senator Tabor and his new wife passed us here. She was dressed in black satin, court train, low corsage and trimmed with three narrow flounces at the bottom of the skirt. She wore a jet capote with a long crape veil falling nearly to the bottom of her dress, and three waving golden curls hung upon her shoulders. The madame wears Langtry bangs, too, her eyes are large, of a deep, pansy hue, and she is what might be called an Irish beauty. Tabor himself, is a cross between an Arizona cowboy and a Mollie Maguire— great dark eyes and features, he looks vindictive and hateful. But his handsome nightshirts, his big diamonds, that ten million bank account, were a great temptation to an obscure beauty like Miss McCourt.

A WEDDING HAS BEEN ARRANGED

Father Chapelle of St. Matthew's Church, says he did not know that Tabor was divorced or he would not have married them in the Catholic communion.

Even the columns of the *Police Gazette* described the new Mrs. Tabor, at the same time publishing the most flattering drawing of Augusta. The latter liked it so much that she pasted it, together with another of Horace, in her scrapbook. She discarded the third drawing—the one of Baby Doe. The *Police Gazette* caption declared, "Lizzie McCourt is a tall, finely-built woman, possessing a charm best expressed in the French word, *plantureuse*. She has turned many a young man's head in her time and certainly has entirely captured the Senator."

Another Washington correspondent further extolled Baby Doe's beauty when he declared,

> *She is a perfect blonde, with a magnificent suit of golden hair which he (Tabor) assures me reaches nearly to the floor when uncoiled. I should say that there never was a more beautiful set of teeth than the smile which parting her lips discloses, while her eyes are large and full of expression. Her nose is slightly retroussé, but that only adds to the piquancy of a face that would be called beautiful among beauties.*

Baby Doe was very much in evidence on the occasion of her husband's last day as Senator, for she sat prominently in the Senate's ladies' gallery, wearing a gown of brown silk with a tight-fitting bodice that did full justice to her voluptuous form. With necklace, earrings and bracelets of glittering diamonds, she excited the admiration of many a normal American senator below. Around her waist was an unusual "jeweled waist-girdle in the shape of a serpent, with diamond eyes, ruby tongue and long tail of emeralds." She was fully aware that the senators were whispering about her—something she loved, for Baby Doe Tabor was a most womanly woman. Adulation in so high a place was enough to turn the head of any ordinary young woman from Oshkosh, Wisconsin.

Tabor was still boasting that he was coming back to Washington, where he would build the most handsome house in the city "and furnish it like Vanderbilt." As reported in the *State Register* on March 7, he was "very proud of his young wife, her sealskin jacket, her diamond bracelets, and pointed out to Senators on the floor the other expensive articles of her toilette."

Some of the more sophisticated senators called him a "donkey" because he went among them collecting their autographs in a special album, while at home the Denver *Tribune* enjoyed a Field day at Tabor's expense:

> *Special advices from Washington agree that yesterday was the most exciting day ever witnessed in the United States Senate. It terminated the Honorable H.A.W. Tabor's career in that august body . . . Early in the day the streets were alive with people hurry-*

Sarah Bernhardt, a favorite dinner guest.

Oscar Wilde. He lectured on practical aesthetics and descended into the mine for supper, "the first course being whisky, the second whisky and the third whisky."

Baby Doe's $7,000 wedding gown and [inset] Tabor's famous gold watch fob — relics of memorable first nights.

Tabor Grand Opera House, Denver. Inside: crimson plush, and 1500 pendants on the chandelier.

Silver Dollar Tabor being presented to Theodore Roosevelt, August 29, 1910. William Jennings Bryan gave her the name.

Silver Dollar, Baby's favorite daughter and beloved "Honey-maid."

The end of a fabulous story. Interior of cabin by the Matchless Mine.

A rare visit to Denver. "I had all the enjoyment I wanted when I was young. I do not need enjoyment now!"

ing to the Capitol. Flags were hung at half-mast . . . The galleries were filled to overflowing with the most beautiful and accomplished ladies of the Republic and the floor of the Senate was crowded with eminent persons.

When Senator Tabor entered the room, bearing a new patent-leather grip-sack and wearing a superb trousseau of broadcloth and diamonds, the vast crowd was as hushed as the grave. Senator Sherman submitted a series of resolutions lamenting Tabor's departure. It was unanimously adopted, Senator Tabor maintaining his characteristic modesty to the last and abstaining from voting. The Senator rose to speak. As he proceeded to recount his services, love of country, and devotion to the public weal, men groaned in speechless agony and whole platoons of police were kept busy carrying insensible ladies from the galleries. . . .

At night there was a torchlight parade in ex-Senator Tabor's honor. It was an imposing affair, numbering 12,000 persons in line and the entire American Navy on wheels, and was gorgeously illuminated. The crowning feature of the procession was a huge papier-maché yacht, representing the Ship of State and manned by forty-one beautiful young girls, representing the States and Territories, from Oshkosh.

Completely unaware of Eugene Field's romancing, and in any case too much in love to let it bother them, the newlyweds entrained for a wedding trip to New York before returning to Denver.

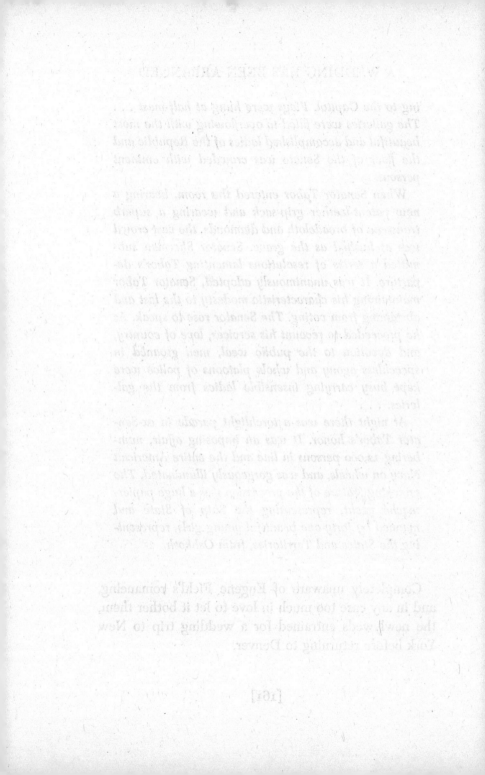

Chapter Eight

The Happy Home

TWO wives in one city might have daunted a lesser man than H.A.W. Tabor. He did not turn a hair even when he heard that their rival carriages had raced each other through the streets, each wife urging her coachman to drive "faster, faster." It annoyed him far more that nobody called upon the second Mrs. Tabor, although, as her scrapbook of begging letters proves, every philanthropic and charitable group in Denver wrote her for contributions. Unfortunately for her own pocket, Baby Doe had a big heart and usually responded.

Early in April she was to make her first public appearance in Denver, the city that had benefited so much from Tabor's generosity. Sensational as the day Baby stole the Senate limelight, this time the scene was set at the Tabor Grand Opera House where the great American tragedian, Lawrence Barrett, was portraying Cardinal Richelieu. A large and appreciative audience was following the most minute movements of the red-robed man onstage when suddenly the excited whisper, "Baby Doe," passed like a soft wind through the waves of silk and satin.

Immediately every lorgnette in the house was focused on the special Tabor box, and there she was—the siren, the hussy, the creature who had done poor Augusta wrong. If they expected to see a gaudily overdressed and painted creature the ladies were painfully disappointed, for Baby Doe Tabor had chosen to wear a simple black gown with a neat black bonnet that nestled prettily upon her reddish-gold curls. She did not have a single jewel or other form of adornment.

Wearing a severe Prince Albert coat, Tabor stood proudly at her side, accompanied by Peter McCourt, Baby's brother, the epitome of fashion in his dandyish clothes. Two ushers carried into the box four bouquets in blue vases, from one of which Baby Doe plucked a white calla lily, playing with it for the rest of the evening. Never in his entire career had Mr. Barrett played against such keen competition as the new Mrs. Tabor with her emblem of purity! Later he was somewhat placated by receiving a large floral star, four and one-half feet high, comprising a solid mass of forget-me-nots, immortelles, Bon Silene roses, Japan lilies, white roses, pinks and white daisies. The word BARRETT was picked out in scarlet geraniums. A card accompanying the lavish floral tribute bore the simple inscription *Compliments of Mrs. H.A.W. Tabor.*

Next day the temperamental tragedian thought the fading flowers poor consolation for his wounded pride when he read in the press that "Mr. Barrett was playing Richelieu as a merely incidental feature of the evening."

Safe now from the prying eyes of the first Mrs. Tabor, who had sold her interest in the venture, the newlyweds had settled temporarily in a palatial suite at the Windsor Hotel. Two German athletic societies who had serenaded them upon their return from Washington were really the only organizations friendly to the newlyweds. At a banquet Tabor was praised as being one of the first Americans to associate himself with those whose aims were "to educate our youth not only in physical, but also in moral development."

On May 14, 1883, Peter McCourt, Senior, Baby Doe's father, died, casting a shadow upon her new-found happiness, for the McCourts had always been a warmly affectionate family. Still Denver society did not receive her, the only occasions upon which she was welcomed being industrial banquets and official receptions. In contrast Augusta, although as a "divorced woman" feeling an acute personal stigma, was invited everywhere.

Several conflicting stories are told of Augusta's sinking her pride to call on Baby, since her calling card was found years later among Baby's belongings. Augusta is said to have thought that if, for Tabor's sake, she called upon her rival, others would follow her example. However, it is hard to believe that she did; such an action seems inconsistent with Augusta's proud nature and completely at variance with the bitter statements about Tabor and Baby Doe that she gave out to the newspapers.

If Denver was cold, lusty Leadville was just the opposite. No reigning monarch could have received more adulation than the Silver Queen of Colorado when she visited the Cloud City. She was met, with her "king," at the railroad station by the brightly uniformed Tabor Light Cavalry, and a sixteen-piece band played them all the way to a champagne reception at the Clarendon hotel. Every bona fide lady and every soiled dove in the mountain metropolis was eager to catch a glimpse of Baby Doe's rubies and diamonds.

On July 25 the *Rocky Mountain News* described the Tabors' arrival to attend the 17th Annual Encampment of the Grand Army of the Republic parade in Denver. By this time some Colorado husbands were getting tired of hearing from their envious wives about Baby Doe and the wonderful things her husband was doing for her.

Few events attracted more attention from the on-

*lookers than the ex-Senator's magnificent new coach,
drawn by four splendid brown horses, wearing heavy
gold-mounted harness. A colored coachman in a gorgeous crimson and old gold livery held the reins over
the four-in-hand, and a colored footman, equally resplendent in a livery to match, sat by the coachman
when the coach was in motion and tended the door
with stately dignity when the coach stopped.*

*Inside the spacious vehicle sat Senator Tabor in the
full and striking uniform of the Tabor Light Cavalry,
of Leadville. His brother-in-law, Mr. Peter McCourt,
sat beside him in citizen's clothes, and on the opposite seat were Mrs. Tabor and her mother, Mrs.
McCourt, both dressed in deep mourning.*

*The turn-out attracted a great deal of attention, as
it was the first appearance of the $3000 coach which
has been so much talked of. Mr. Tabor said he desired to honor the day, and was much pleased with
the furore caused by the team, coach and liveried
servants. He will drive in state to the Exposition this
afternoon . . .*

*The handsome liveries worn by Senator Tabor's
coachman and footman were made by Appel & Co.
They are of scarlet jersey, trimmed with silver lace,
and were designed by E.S. Bertram, manager of the
custom department of the house.*

Upon his return to Denver, Tabor boasted that he
was sending to Honduras, where he had vast forestry
investments, for mahogany to build Baby Doe a
mansion the like of which the city had never seen; but
he became too involved in other projects to carry out

his plan. Instead, he bought a house firmly constructed of brick at 1647 Welton Street. Although it was a fine house, it was not elaborate enough to serve his taste for long.

In the autumn the name of Tabor was again front-page news, for on October 17 *The Statesman*, described on its masthead as "an Independent National Journal published at Bayonne, New Jersey," began to boost Tabor as a possible Republican candidate.

Concerning Tabor's capabilities *The Statesman* said:

REPUBLICAN
FOR PRESIDENT
OF THE UNITED STATES,
HORACE A.W. TABOR
OF DENVER, COLORADO.

Silver King of the Pacific Slope.
Colorado's honest Citizen, Banker
and Senator, of sterling talent and
purity of character.

An Independent statesman upholding the
Constitution and Union.

A foe to monopoly and centralization of a
money power endangering Liberty.

Favoring a gold and silver currency
and protection to the manufacturing
interests of the Country.

THE HAPPY HOME

The champion of the working man.

A new light from the ranks of the people.

Tabor would rather have first served a term as Governor of Colorado, leaving his Presidential aspirations for later. On the other hand, Baby Doe, showered on every side by gifts from her doting husband, already dreamed of becoming America's First Lady and living in fitting grandeur at the White House. She wondered what Mama Doe and her arch-enemy, the total abstainer Mrs. Belford, would say then.

Denver residents had hardly recovered from the shock of having "Ex-Senator Nightshirt," as the wags called Tabor, suggested as the next First Executive when they heard that a violent quarrel had broken out between him and Bush, his Man Friday. Baby Doe, who had never forgotten his insults in Central City, had managed to persuade her husband that the dapper, elegantly attired Peter McCourt (Pete), her younger brother, should replace Bush as his manager.

Tabor, on his part, was jealous of the fatherly influence Bush wielded over young Maxcy who, since the divorce, had left his father's services, completely siding with Augusta. In a suit against Bush, Tabor accused his erstwhile friend of embezzling the sum of $2,000. Bush was acquitted, retaliating by telling the Supreme Court that Tabor owed him $100,000 for various services rendered. For seeking testimony and witnesses to procure the Durango divorce (which Tabor had publicly declared never took place), and for persuading Augusta at last to divorce her husband, Bush asked $10,000. As for "aiding him in effecting a marriage with the said Mrs. Doe, commonly called Baby Doe" (how Bush enjoyed thrusting this final dart at the new Mrs. Tabor!) he demanded an even larger sum. Finally he wanted $1,547 as reimbursement for bribes allegedly paid to legislators during the senatorial election, the sums varying from $5 to $475. Augusta, who was subpoenaed to give evidence, found herself unwillingly caught in the middle of this bitter quarrel.

Baby Doe was not alone in her dislike of Bush; Augusta had no real love for him either. Maxcy was her only son and she resented the influence Bush held over him. Reluctantly Augusta set out for the court-room, which was filled with many a Denver lady curious only to hear what she would say. As it turned out, Augusta gave them their full money's worth, collecting her own full pound of flesh.

The headlines in the Denver *Times* for October 29 made strange bedfellows, for they simply announced:

MR. BUSH AND MRS. TABOR
They Create Quite a Sensation in Court

They certainly did; and with Judge Teller presiding, Augusta's victory was complete. In the middle of the case, in walked Tabor, somewhat startled at seeing Augusta sitting aloft in the witness stand while the opposing lawyers were squabbling as to her competency as a witness. While this was going on Augusta's eyes fixed themselves on Tabor's white face like those of a hen-hawk. At last he could stand them no longer, turning his chair towards the wall.

The highlight of the proceedings, according to the Denver *Tribune* report, came when in cross-examination Augusta testified that the last time Bush called upon her was on April 28, 1882, when he was trying to buy the furniture in the Windsor Hotel.

"Then Mr. Bush never called on you in reference to the divorce after April, 1882," asked lawyer Patterson.

It was then that Augusta dropped her bombshell.

"I have never been divorced," she declared triumphantly. "I am still his wife."

"Yes, we know that," Patterson placated her before a buzz of excited feminine lips disrupted the court.

Bush's charges against Tabor, who for the occasion of the trial wore a plum-colored coat chosen by Peter McCourt, were struck from the record as being "indecent and irrelevant." The two men were never friends again. In the end Tabor actually obtained a judgment for $19,958 against his former Man Friday.

Augusta had her own troubles. She was sued for refusing to pay the "exorbitant" fees of lawyers Wells, Smith and Macon for procuring the divorce that she now refused to recognize. At a jury hearing the plaintiffs found their charges reduced to $2,817, which with interest compiling at ten per cent from the previous January gave them a total sum of $3,036.05. Even then Augusta thought they had been given far too much.

Although supposedly sick to death of lawyers and publicity, Augusta had no qualms in granting a Denver *Republican* reporter a juicy interview on October 31:

STILL TABOR'S WIFE
Interview with Mrs. Tabor No. 1, in Which
She Makes Some Spicy Revelations

This time she had no headache as when the previous reporter called. She was "seated in an elegant, almost luxuriously furnished sitting room" making a patchwork pincushion, "a prey to silent reflections, thinking of one she helped to elevate . . . of one who deserted her after she had grown faded in working for him."

Augusta's face might have grown faded, but not her tongue, which was tarter than ever.

"I have been reading something about Mr. Tabor," she said, without giving her visitor the chance to open the questioning. "I know you want to talk about him and me. Well, there has been scandal enough, God knows; but I do not think I have been scorched much in passing through the fire. It has aged me though—the shock was terrible."

The reporter asked whether she had begun proceedings to set aside the second divorce in spite of the fact that Tabor had remarried, and also mentioned that her friends maintained she had sacrificed herself by divorcing him properly in Denver only to save him from bigamy charges stemming from the St. Louis marriage. In reply Augusta confessed, "Not yet; I hardly know what to do. I do not consider myself divorced from Mr. Tabor . . ."

Later, when asked if she thought Tabor would leave Baby Doe and return to live with her, Augusta sadly admitted, "No, I couldn't hope for that; but it would be a great satisfaction to me to know that the woman would be no more to him than she was before he gave her his name and mine. I understand that she has all her family quartered at his home. I mean all in this country. I understand that a fresh invoice is coming over from Ireland. I have never seen her, but I know she has seen me, for I have heard of it. [*Augusta seems conveniently to have forgotten her spying on the veiled Baby Doe at the Windsor Hotel.*] She is a blonde, I understand, and paints. Mr. Tabor has changed a great deal. He used to detest women of that kind. He would never allow me to whitewash my face, however much I desired to do so. She wants his money and will hang on to him as long as he has got a nickel. She don't want an old man."

The reporter drew a sharp look from Augusta when he ventured to suggest that Mr. Tabor was not such an old man.

"Oh yes, he is," insisted Augusta. "He dyes his hair and mustache. I noticed him in the courtroom the other day. He was afraid to draw his handkerchief across his mouth for fear of staining it. I also noticed that the hair on his temples, which is gray, was covered nicely, giving him a rejuvenated appearance."

Augusta paused, carefully adjusting her pince-nez spectacles, then continued, "I see but very little of Mr. Tabor now. He never comes by here. The other day in the courtroom was the first I had seen of him for a good while. I wanted to get a good look at him, and I did," she confessed, obviously with much satisfaction. "As I was coming down the stairs with Mr. Teller I overtook him at the door and spoke. He seemed horrified and looked indignant, but made no reply. He would not have had me do it for the world, but I couldn't help it. He is very farsighted, and whenever he sees me will hurry away in an opposite direction. I cannot help but feel gratified that he and Bush are at loggerheads."

Later she told the reporter of the arrival of her aged father-in-law from Vermont.

"By the way, Mr. Tabor's father is here," she said. "It's a wonder he doesn't come to see me. I know him well and nursed him once when he was sick. I suppose the Senator has poisoned his mind against me, as he has everybody else's—at least his relatives." She paused. "He keeps him at McCourt's. If he were stopping at the hotel I would go to see him." Then suddenly

Augusta laughed. "Are there really seventeen in that McCourt family? There is one thing Mr. Tabor cannot say, and that is that any of my relatives ever received a cent from him." She shrugged her shoulders before adding emphatically, "That woman will break him up."

"You cannot say, then, when you will commence proceedings," prompted the reporter, trying to goad her into an answer.

"No, but I will let you know," promised Augusta. "I told you when you came in that I had been reading about Senator Tabor. I preserve everything I see about him. I have three scrapbooks full. When I first commenced saving clippings from newspapers I saved nothing but the articles speaking well of him. It used to make me mad to read anything derogatory to his character, but I soon saw that I would have to see the dark as well as the bright side, so I preserved everything." She pursed her lips triumphantly, like the cat who has at last eaten the canary. "My last scrapbook is full of scandal, nothing but scandal. It would make a big volume if put in book form. That was a splendid thing of Mr. Field's about the McCourt family coming to Denver. I read that occasionally when I am feeling dispirited and want a good laugh."

In spite of her threats Augusta did not move to upset the divorce for two reasons: first, she would have had to return her settlement, and secondly, there was her son Maxcy's future to be thought of. Maxcy was about to marry a most respectable young woman, Luella Babcock, and the scandal concerning the name of Tabor was not particularly attractive. Augusta decided to bide her time, certain that, after getting all she could from her elderly husband, Baby Doe would leave him for a younger man.

Maxcy's wedding took place on January 17, 1884, prior to which Augusta penned the following document to H.A.W. Tabor . . .

> *Mr. Tabor, Sir:*
>
> *OUR son is to be married the 17th. You have promised me that he should be well provided for financially. You also told Mr. Rockwell* [the attorney] *. . . the same thing. Now something has to be done for him. You certainly cannot expect me to help him from the penurious mite that I received. So from your abundance I entreat you to help him.*
>
>

Your wife,

AUGUSTA L. TABOR.

The letter found a place in Baby Doe's scrapbook. How Tabor responded to the appeal from the woman he had put aside is a matter for conjecture. He was always a generous man, so it would be unfair to assume him otherwise on this occasion involving his own son. He is said to have given Maxcy $50,000 for a business stake.

The newspaper coverage of the wedding was surprisingly brief, considering the mountains of print that had been issued about the second wedding of the bridegroom's father. The Denver *Republican* on January 17, 1884, announced briefly under the heading LOCAL that "The Tabor-Babcock Wedding will occur at noon today." The following day on page four the actual nuptials merited only one line: "LOCAL—N. M. Tabor was married to Miss Lou Babcock."

The Rocky Mountain News published the following brief account on page four, column four, of their January 18, 1884, issue:

> *The marriage of Mr. N.M. Tabor, son of the ex-Senator, and Miss Lou Babcock, occurred at the home of the bride, on Champa street at 5 o'clock last evening. Rev. Dr. Reuben Jeffrey and Rev. Dr. A.M. Weeks officiated. But a few of the immediate relatives of the families were present, and the presents were of a magnificent and costly character. After the bridal dinner the bride and groom left the city at 7 o'clock for a tour to the East.*

It is interesting to note that although he and his father had recently fallen out, Maxcy is described as the "son of the ex-Senator," while there is no mention of Augusta. Tabor's wives were both prone to self-effacement where Horace was concerned.

On January 24, while Maxcy and Luella were respectably honeymooning in St. Louis, Denver society exploded with the news that Augusta Louise Tabor had eloped with a handsome, red-haired young book sales-man from Philadelphia! Even Tabor could hardly believe what he read in the daily newspapers. The Denver *Tribune* went so far as to announce the fact from its office window. Unfortunately Augusta was not on hand either to confirm or deny that she had made a sudden trip to the altar. According to friends she had left Denver the previous Tuesday, intending to join the newlyweds in St. Louis, before traveling South, there to embark on a health trip to Cuba.

According to a New York *Herald* report, William Artman, the "bridegroom," had turned up a few weeks previously in Denver where he at once distinguished himself as "a wonderful story teller."

> *He said he had been with Stanley when the latter was sent out by the* Herald *to find Livingstone, and he claimed to be on intimate terms with all the crowned heads of Europe. He added that he ex-pected soon to be commissioned to discover the South Pole. Among others whom he visited in the town was Mrs. Tabor. A few days ago he appeared in a new mood and a new suit. In fact he said he was going to be married, and it was rumored that he was heard to mention that the lady had money. Suddenly he disappeared, and it was on a Tuesday.*

Friends "in a position to know" insisted that Augusta had indeed married the traveling salesman at 2:30 the very afternoon she had embarked for St. Louis. This was quickly denied by the Reverend A. M. Weeks, who was one of her boarders and pastor of the same Unitarian Church where Augusta was a staunch member. He was most upset, declaring that surely she would have allowed him to perform the ceremony were she contemplating matrimony. (There had already been one false rumor that Augusta was to marry a young Unitarian minister ten years her junior.)

Unfortunately for many Denver residents who, on the strength of his "secret engagement" to the rich Denver divorcée, had loaned "the bridegroom" money, Augusta—still in a single state—was finally found to be staying on Canal Street, New Orleans. Quickly she informed the press that

> *"I desired to get away from the cold weather, and determined to go to Cuba. I would have gone via New York, but I came to New Orleans to avoid the cold. I will go from here to Cuba, and then to Florida, and from there I will go North. I wouldn't certainly run away from home to get married. When I do get married I will do so openly and above board. If I do marry you can be certain it will not be Mr. Artman. I will not marry a man whom I will have to support but will expect my husband to support me. It may be that Artman started the rumor himself. The dispatch says he borrowed money on the strength of the wedding. If there were any Denver people who were fools enough to believe me so foolish, I'm glad that they were duped."*

Upon Augusta's return from her travels she was to receive another shock, this time one that probably influenced her decision not to proceed with the threat to annul the Denver divorce.

Baby Doe was expecting a baby.

Although she secretly longed for a son to replace the one she had lost when married to Harvey, Baby felt that she had to bear Tabor a son as Augusta had done. She was bitterly disappointed when at the Welton street mansion she gave birth to a girl. However, this feeling was soon dispersed when she saw the joy that Tabor found in his new daughter. Immediately he had a gold medallion struck, bearing on one side the inscription:

BABY TABOR
July 13
1884

and on the other,

Compliments of the Tabor Guards,
Boulder, Colorado

It was the size of a twenty-five cent piece.

The press seems to have had a change of heart with the advent of the little girl, especially when her doting father entertained all the reporters at the opera house. Even the Catholic Church, which the Tabors had offended so much by the Washington wedding, showed its friendliness. Upon hearing of Tabor's medallion, Father Guida, rector of the Church of the Sacred Heart, Denver, whose calling card appears in one of Baby Doe's scrapbooks, sent along one of his own with the note, "Here is a somewhat better badge of consecration for the baby . . . It is also a silver medal, blessed by the Holy Father in Rome."

This gesture on the part of the kindly priest pleased Baby Doe more than any of the more expensive gifts bestowed upon her infant. Falling out with the Church had caused her more personal suffering than any blow inflicted by feminine acquaintances.

Religious matters had not improved when Tabor had refused a certain Monsignor Capel permission to lecture in the Grand Opera House, Denver, on "The Infallibility of the Pope" because Bishop Machebeuf, Augusta's old friend, whom she had nursed through a severe attack of mountain fever years before, had refused to rent Baby Doe and himself a pew in St. Mary's Cathedral.

Baby Doe hoped that with the arrival of her child all this ill-feeling would be forgotten, for now her only desire was to become a good wife and mother. "My own cup of bliss was overflowing for some time," she said, "and I forgot all about the jealous cats and sanctimonious old battle-axes of Denver. I was a mother!"

No fairy princess could have been given a more elaborate christening than the little Tabor child. She was taken to Oshkosh, Baby Doe's home town, with a wardrobe of over fifty beautiful tiny gowns made of silk, lace and velvet. Even the gold pins used to fasten her baby clothes were set with real diamonds. The actual christening gown was partially made of Honiton lace, "the two flounces on the robe costing $500 apiece." A cloak of white embroidered velvet was edged with point lace and marabou tips. "Her tiny French felt hat was heavy with marabou tips, each one of which cost not less than $10." The entire outfit cost over $15,000. The bootees were specially made for the occasion, as was the miniature jeweled necklace complete with locket.

Grandma McCourt was overwhelmed with pride at the arrival of her granddaughter Lizzie Bonduel Lillie. Her triumph would have been complete had Mama Doe been among the congregation, but even if she wasn't, there was some consolation in counting the crowd of fellow townsfolk who had turned out to witness the most fabulous christening Oshkosh had ever seen.

Mrs. Harriet Wilkerson had embroidered Lillie's robe, asking $100 for the work. "Not nearly enough," insisted Baby Doe, pressing fifteen brand new gold pieces into her hand. The latter had sent to New York for the intricate embroidery transfer designs in the middle of which were the initials B.T., signifying "Baby Tabor." How Augusta winced when her well-meaning friends related every tiny detail. It was bad enough to read in the newspaper that "fortune has again smiled upon ex-Senator Tabor. All is sunshine and gladness at his home."

At the Denver Exposition Tabor carried Lillie in his arms down the center aisle with the second Mrs. Tabor by his side. Around the world the baby was fêted as the "Little Silver Princess," her photographs being widely distributed both in Europe and her native America. When Thomas Nast, the famed artist, later to become U.S. Consul-General at Guayaquil, Ecuador, visited Denver he was so enchanted with Lillie—then described as "the most photographed baby in the world" and "always posing herself without assistance"—that he sketched her for the cover jacket of *Harper's Weekly*. With much pride Baby Doe saved a clipping for her scrapbook: "The demand in the city for the number of *Harper's Weekly* containing Baby Tabor's picture was so great that the supply soon was exhausted."

Newspapers were to carry items when the fortunate Lillie, who had almost literally been born with a silver spoon in her mouth, cut her first tooth, took her first step and won her first prize at kindergarten. Baby was determined that this child should have everything money could buy, especially since she would have to associate with the children and grandchildren of the very matrons who had ostracized her mother.

Nast noticed the beautiful Baby Doe as well as her offspring, for upon leaving Denver he gave her his photograph signed TH. NAST. It shows him as a handsome man with a forked beard, wearing a magnificent square stickpin.

Lily, her elderly father's idol, continued to prosper. A photograph exists of the top-hatted Tabor (his familiar stovepipe seems to be missing upon this important family occasion) sitting in a high horse-drawn buggy with baby Lillie dandled upon his knee. As an infant she seldom cried. Upon reaching the toddler stage she visited the theater, "capering all through the play in her father's box," the latter newly upholstered in pure white satin in honor of Baby Doe.

These were happy days for Tabor and his beloved. With pride he read in the Wednesday July 16, 1884, *Owl,*

> *The Tabor Grand Opera House of Denver, is truly a grand building but it is not singular in that respect, nor an exotic grafted upon a less regal plant. It is simply in keeping with the architectural requirements of the Town, and an exponent of the spirit and culture of its people. A less elegant opera house would not have satisfied the public, and would have brought its builder censure instead of gratitude. Luckily Mr. Tabor was in full sympathy with the aspirations of the people of Denver, and while his work stands, it will be a monument not only to his public spirit, but to his enlightened intelligence and good sense.*

As his wife kept telling him, "You have helped to make Denver known in other parts of the world."

At least Baby's table was graced with the beauties and famed actors of the theatre, including Lily Langtry, Lillian Russell, Sarah Bernhardt, Mme. Modjeska, Edwin Booth, Otis Skinner, William Gillette, Augustin Daly and John Drew.

Baby Doe particularly liked Sarah Bernhardt, and the feeling was mutual. Oscar Wilde had dubbed the actress the "Divine Sarah" after she had played in London in 1879, so she was intrigued to hear the story told at Baby Doe's table of his descent into Tabor's Matchless Mine. After that, Baby clipped every mention of her divine guest she could ever find, including a delightful one from the *Cincinnati Inquirer* that read, "Sarah's dresses this year are simply indescribable for splendor and yet, do you know, she is still wearing some of those she had with her in America—for instance, that dark blue plush she wore in 'Frou-Frou,' that still lives; also a splendid red embossed velvet she wore in 'Camille.' In those days Baby Doe was extremely fashion-conscious. Sometimes she laughed quietly with Tabor because her enemies imitated her choice of dress! The air of happiness continued to hang over Tabor Home Number Two, despite the fact that the occupant of Tabor Home Number One was still very much in evidence. Lawyer Amos Steck had been right when he said of Augusta, "She is crazy about Tabor. She loves him and that settles it."

That still settled it. If only Augusta had been able to put Tabor out of her mind, life might still have been beautiful. Unfortunately she couldn't! In October, 1885, an East-bound passenger meeting Augusta for the first time left this pen picture of her:

I've just been out in Denver and while there I met Mrs. Tabor, divorced wife of the nightshirt senator. She has not married again, but is living quietly with her son. [Maxcy and Luella started their married lives together as guests in Augusta's home.] *She has developed very good business tact, and has taken such admirable care of the $400,000 which she got from her husband that she is now a millionaire. Tabor, on the other hand, has been gradually going down hill. Not long ago he made a rather lucky hit in some mines which revived his drooping fortunes a bit, but the prediction is freely made that in a few years he will flatten out into hopeless bankruptcy. Mrs. Tabor No. 1 says that she will have to take care of "the old man," as come it will, he will find himself deserted by No. 2, and that he will be glad enough to return to his first love and her million. It seems to be the height of this woman's ambition to get her husband back and to be able to set him up again financially.*

Apart from its reference to Augusta's certainty that in the end Tabor would return to her, this item is noteworthy, mentioning as it does his slipping finances. Once before, in 1882, he had been the victim of premature speculation about his money matters. At that time a reliable newspaper had actually accused him of being insolvent. In any case, Augusta didn't intend to let Tabor pass from her life forever. She was certain that one day he would lose his fortune and Baby Doe would leave him.

A letter written by a Denver correspondent to the *Utica Observer* at this period describes Augusta as having "a high forehead, dark-brown hair, black eyes and remarkably intelligent features . . . Her tones were low and her English was of the purest."

Baby's and Augusta's Christmas celebrations are worth comparing. After Lillie was born, it was Baby's habit on Christmas Eve to set out in her grand coach to visit the poorer sections of Denver, where she bountifully distributed foods, fowls, money and toys. Extravagant in her personal tastes, she was at all times generous to those less fortunate than herself and she enjoyed her annual role of Lady Bountiful.

The poor were not the only recipients of Baby Doe's gifts; anybody who showed her a kindness often received one in return. All her life she preserved a letter from Ella Hoyle Beck with its notepaper heading, "Supreme Court Chambers, Denver."

> *The bottle of lovely perfumery left at my room on Saturday reached me safely, and you are the best thing that lives. I hope when you get to heaven they will give you a front row in the dress circle and let you pick out your own harp!*

At Augusta's mansion there was usually an "at home" for the favored friends and young people. On one such occasion the house was decorated with Christmas greens and its alcoves were filled with palms and ferns. Luella had decked with candles and fairy lamps the rather gloomy library, where at ten o'clock the young folk were allowed to dance. Augusta was resplendent in "an elegant long gown of gold and white brocade, one side of it covered with claret-colored plush under Duchesse point lace." Luella wore "a long décolleté gown of white silk and crystal lace." The ladies, including the wife of the Governor of Colorado, were in "elegant street dress, or full evening toilets." Even the Governor attended Augusta's parties.

In the summer, Augusta's beautiful tree-shaded lawns were much sought after by her church for strawberry and ice-cream parties. In spite of what she termed "the ignominious stigma of divorce" she was once chosen to chaperone a group of girls on an educational picnic to South Cheyenne canyon.

Chapter Nine

The Beginning of the End

"THE hospitality and beauty of the West amazes me." As he spoke General William Tecumseh Sherman stared into Baby Doe's pansy-blue eyes. The famous veteran of the War between the States had thoroughly enjoyed his visit to Leadville where he had been royally entertained by Mr. and Mrs. H.A.W. Tabor. They had borrowed Dave Moffat's private car and had traveled by Denver and South Park railroad to the Cloud City especially to meet him. At a champagne party held in the General's honor at the Clarendon Hotel, Tabor had engaged a special orchestra, composed entirely of miners, to play. After a tour of the silver mines, entertainment was enjoyed at the Tabor Opera House, where the Tabor box was filled with Baby Doe's favorite calla lilies.

Back at Denver in December, 1886, Tabor gave $54,000 to purchase the fine Joseph Watson house at Olive (now East 13th Avenue) and Sherman as "a more fitting home for my beloved wife." Inside, the rooms were overstuffed in the late-Victorian manner. A fountain played in a main reception room, its little pool surrounded by an attractive metal grille. On the floors only the finest oriental rugs and carpets were used, while the drapes were of heavy plush and silk brocade. Costly oil paintings hung on the walls, and Tabor had commissioned six portraits to be painted of his wife alone. From the ceilings were suspended real crystal chandeliers. Even the White House, Baby Doe thought, could not be more lavishly furnished.

A flight of steps led up to the terrace where the two main entrances were supported by graceful pillars. On the lawns stood bronze deer and staghounds cast in a Parisian foundry.

There were also the scandalous nude statues which today would not be noticed. In response to a complaint from a prudish neighbor, Baby Doe with Irish prankishness solved the problem in her own way. She dressed Nimrod in scarlet hunting boots and a prim Derby hat; Psyche in white satin, and Diana, Goddess of Hunting and Chastity, in transparent gossamer chiffon complete with lingerie.

THE BEGINNING OF THE END

Baby Doe's brother, Peter McCourt, as the new manager of the Denver Tabor Grand Opera House, was now given his big opportunity to make good. Often Peter, who moved in high society, brought young men to dine at Baby Doe's table. Once, when Tabor was away on business, Baby Doe could stand the insult no longer. Marching downstairs, she told the startled stag-party that even if she was deemed not good enough for the mothers, her food did not seem to poison their sons. Furious though Peter was at her outburst, he could not deny that his own success had come about only because of his sister.

It was when Tabor was away that Baby Doe's sense of loneliness and nonacceptance was most pronounced. Perhaps that was why he wrote her daily, while she sent him poems of her own composition.

As a postscript to one particular offering she added

> *(Stop that nose business)*
> *Nice Sweet 'B' flat*
> *Clairnette* [clarinette]
> Kiss.

The "nose business" may have referred to her little tiptilted nose—the only blemish in her otherwise classic features—about which he often teased her.

On October 17, 1888, Baby Doe gave birth to a son, Horace Joseph, but her joy was cut short when after ten hours the infant died. On top of the small white casket was a silver plate describing the child as "son of H.A.W. Tabor." Baby Doe is not mentioned. The loss of this second boy (the first she had borne to Harvey Doe) was a source of much grief to her, for she still longed to give Tabor a son, as Augusta had done. Baby Doe failed to understand why she, a woman in such good health, could not bear a healthy son.

Almost immediately she became pregnant again, and a second daughter arrived on December 17, 1889. Wearing an $800 gown, the child was fantastically christened Rose Mary Echo Silver Dollar Tabor. William Jennings Bryan, the great orator, then a young man, named her when he exclaimed, "Why, Senator, that baby's laughter has the ring of a silver dollar!" This was Baby Doe's favorite daughter—her beloved "Honeymaid."

But along with this extra domestic blessing the Tabors' life of luxury was fast approaching a bitter end. There were several causes, of which the decline in the price of silver took precedence. During his second term in office President Grover Cleveland repealed the 1890 Sherman Silver Purchase Act, restoring the sinking gold reserve. William Jennings Bryan, who for some years had studied the currency question, especially in connection with the position of silver currency, had tried unsuccessfully to impress Tabor—popularly believed to be the richest silver mine owner in the West—that if and when the gold standard men in the East pitted themselves against the silver men of the West, the entire United States economy would be imperiled.

Tabor, to his later chagrin, did not take seriously Bryan's timely warning. Had he done so, the Tabor saga might have ended on a far happier note.

Gradually Tabor's fantastic fortune, valued at from eight to ten million dollars at its peak period, disintegrated to nothing. At the time of the divorce the clever Augusta had listed only her husband's assets—not his net worth or liabilities.

During the years 1884, 1886 and 1888 Tabor ran unsuccessfully for the governorship of Colorado. In addition, during the two latter campaigns he served as chairman of the Republican State Central Committee. His financial contributions to his party's cause were enormous. Even as his investments failed with surprising rapidity one after another he believed with childlike simplicity that the old Tabor luck would renew his fortunes.

With his capital fast disappearing, Tabor struck out with the desperation of a drowning man. Now that the Federal Government was no longer purchasing 4,500,000 ounces of silver a month for making coinage, the price of silver dropped abruptly. The silver mines were idle. On February 29, 1892, the beautiful mansion Tabor had bought so proudly for Baby Doe for $54,000 was mortgaged for $30,000. It was foreclosed in 1896. He even had to borrow money against his beloved Matchless, the one mine in which he had always held an almost fanatical belief.

Liquidation, court suits, mortgaging, loss of prestige

and, what to the Tabors was worst of all—the sinking of their pride—all these trials in turn Baby Doe and he were to know. As a last resort, with their remaining capital, he obtained an option on the Phil Sheridan and Free Coinage group of mines in the new Cripple Creek goldfield, the "$300,000,000 cow pasture" just beyond Pike's Peak. The Tabor luck again failed, although the next owners made millions from the same mines. The Tabor star was really descendent.

In July of 1893, when twelve Denver banks closed their doors, Tabor was penniless, and he had to pawn not only the fabulous jewels he had given to Baby Doe but also those which Jake Sands had given her before the Tabor marriage. Furthermore, in addition to his mining investments, he lost a great deal speculating on the Chicago grain market and in gambling. Although he was a good poker player he was no match for the professionals in Clifton Bell's private gambling room at the Tabor Grand Opera House in Denver. His divorce, high living expenses, generous giving and political contributions had all taken their toll of his vast fortune. He had even bought a yacht in New York—which he never used—on the pretext that it would be useful for taking the children down to see his mahogany forests in Honduras. Actually all that Tabor owned in that country was a 4-10 interest in the Republic of Honduras-Campbell Reduction Company.

What business friends Tabor had disappeared along

with his fortune. Sinking his pride, he went to see an old acquaintance at Colorado Springs, Winfield Scott Stratton, once the carpenter hired to fix the Silver Dollar symbol over Tabor's Bank of Leadville. Although Tabor had dipped into his pocket on dozens of occasions to help men down on their luck, several of whom were now millionaires, Stratton was the only man who remembered.

"Senator Tabor! Sir, I am honored," he exclaimed, welcoming the aging Tabor into his home.

Quietly but earnestly Tabor explained the reason for his visit. He still owned the Eclipse Mine in Boulder county . . . Perhaps with a little help he could develop it . . . And there was always the Matchless. "I always say to Mrs. Tabor, 'Hang on to the Matchless.' "

Stratton wrote him a check for $15,000. Even then Tabor could not accept it as a gift. He insisted upon giving his benefactor a collateral deed to one of his mines in Arizona, which Stratton guessed would be like the others—worthless.

Soon Baby Doe, toiling once more like a man, as she had at the Fourth of July Mine in her Central City days, was at Boulder beside Tabor. Some of the wagging tongues in Denver hung rather limply. What was this they heard—that hussy with her white, manicured hands working like a common miner? Had they— oh, surely not—misjudged her? But Baby Doe had long ceased to worry what people thought. In spite of everything, the years with her beloved Tabor were the richest she had known or ever would know. She had once pasted into her scrapbook a clipping with the heading SHOULD DIVORCED WOMEN BE RECEIVED INTO SOCIETY? "The reasoning that would keep a divorced woman from society would send to prison the merchant who was robbed by his confidential and trusted cashier," the article declared.

Unfortunately, in spite of Baby Doe's loyalty, the Boulder mine proved a failure.

Meanwhile, Augusta was watching Tabor's grim predicament. She had sold her mansion in 1892, moving across the street to the lush new Brown Palace Hotel, where Maxcy, Luella and her old adversary Bill Bush also lived. She was not happy there but was content to wait for her husband's return, each day hearing of some new financial disaster concerning him. Augusta was certain that Baby Doe would leave him, now that the money was going. In the opera *The Ballad of Baby Doe,* "Augusta" has her best scene when, upon being asked to give back to Tabor part of her divorce settlement, she refuses. She intimates that to take her money Tabor would have to sink his pride, and that, still loving him as she does, she cannot take from him the one thing he has left. Fitting and noble as it sounds in the opera, there seems to be no substantiation for this in real life. Augusta was willing to share her fortune with Tabor only if he came back to her forever. She misjudged the character of her rival who, instead of leaving the sinking ship, stayed aboard to be sacrificed with its captain.

THE BEGINNING OF THE END

And as late as September 15, 1893, Tabor, at sixty-three, could still write to Baby Doe a love letter filled with all the ardor of a new-found passion:

> *Jesus Maria,*
> *Chihuahua,*
> *Mexico*

> *My darling, darling wife,*
> *I long to hold you in my arms and whisper my love*
> *and tell you all my plans . . . The mill will be running*
> *in a few days and it will be the finest in Mexico . . .*

Desperately lonely and broken in spirit, with the final realization that Baby Doe had no intention whatsoever of leaving Tabor, Augusta began to fail in health. She had developed a hacking cough; bright pinpoints of color illumined her pinched white cheeks. Tactfully Maxcy and Luella suggested that she should spend the winter of 1894-95 in California where the climate would be mild. Alone she set out upon her last journey, the destination Pasadena. There after only two months of residence her chronic bronchitis was suddenly worsened by an attack of pneumonia, and after four days in bed she died on January 30, with only strangers to attend her at the end.

On making out her death certificate Dr. H.K. Macomber, her physician, spelt her name incorrectly, calling her Agusta L. Tabor. Unconsciously he also wrote her epitaph—not "First Lady of Leadville," but just

"Housewife." Augusta with her simple tastes would have liked that.

Maxcy had his mother's body returned to Denver for burial in Riverside Cemetery. Tabor went off on his own the day of the funeral. For the first time since he had married Baby Doe he had to be alone for a few hours at least.

Augusta's will began, "This, my last will and testament, is made without giving my beloved husband, Horace A.W. Tabor, an interest in the estate of which I die . . ." Although she could not bring herself to help him, to the end he was her "beloved husband." She refers in the will to an agreement made March 28, 1881, and signed by Tabor. It read, "This is to certify that I give my full consent to my wife to will her property to whomever she pleases."

Maxcy was a rich man, for his mother's shrewdness, especially in connection with Denver properties, had paid rich dividends. She left the sum—vast for those days—of $583,220.95. Included among her personal effects were a pair of diamond solitaire earrings valued at $2,000, given her in happier days by Tabor; a $100 bedstead and dresser; a $100 billiard table which she had once bought in a vain attempt to keep Tabor from wandering; a silver cuspidor, and a breast-pin valued at only one dollar—her most precious possession, containing as it did a lock of Tabor's hair clipped when they were first married.

Tabor had scant time to brood over Augusta's passing, for now his most precious material possession with the exception of the Matchless—the Tabor Grand Opera House—was endangered, the opera house which through his foresight had helped make Denver a city of culture in the eyes of the civilized world. In 1896 he lost not only the Opera House but the Tabor block as well. The opera house furnishings were claimed to satisfy a $40,000 chattel mortgage held by Laura D. Swickhimer-Smith, including all the brass spittoons with which the boxes were well supplied and an oil painting entitled "Richelieu and Julie."

Frantically anticipating the loss of his finest creation, Tabor wrote Senator Teller a simple, heart-moving letter begging him to use his influence to save the opera house from falling into the hands of the indomitable Mrs. Swickhimer-Smith who that morning in her determination to acquire it had given him a "very hard" time. The letter began "My Dear Friend," but its contents fell upon stony ears.

Knowing what the Opera House meant to Tabor, Baby Doe begged her brother Peter McCourt, whom she had helped so much, to advance her the money to pay off the mortgage. "I haven't the money, and even if I had, you'd only mortgage it over again for some silly extravagance," was his answer. Baby Doe, whose mansion on Sherman Street had always been a second home to Peter, was shattered by his attitude. She reminded him that at the time of her second marriage her husband had even settled $150,000 upon their father. Peter shrugged his shoulders. To the day he died in 1929 she called him "The Devil" and never forgave him.

Finally came the day she had dreaded, when workmen arrived to cut off the lights and water in their home because the bills for those facilities could not be paid. "Well, tell your bosses how I feel about it," mumbled Tabor, his shoulders bent, his hands in his pockets. He could say no more, his heart was so full—but Baby did! With her blue eyes flashing she strode into the garden to berate them as they left.

"Remind your employers of the many contributions Tabor has made to Denver," she shouted. "Never mind, we will revive the Matchless and then everything will be as it should be again."

Then going indoors she was greeted by a frightened Lillie and the pride of her life, lovable six-year-old Silver. Pretending it was all part of a splendid game she giggled and joked as with lighted candles she led her small family from room to room. They hauled a barrel of drinking water to the mansion from the Old Courthouse pump. Cooking, washing and ironing, Baby Doe pretended not to notice the absence of her servants. Uniformed maids and scarlet-liveried coachmen were now only a beautiful dream. Fondly she recalled the little children running behind her fairy coach as she showered silver coins from the window. Now, so that her own little girl would look neat for school, Baby had to patch Lillie's clothes—Lillie who as a baby had owned fifty gorgeous gowns.

Throughout this time of adversity she was fortified by Tabor's devoted love. "My dear, brave little Baby," he told her, "so trusting, so constant, so hard-working—and always so cheerful. Your love has been the most beautiful thing in my life."

Then even the house was lost and the Tabors moved into cheap rooms. To Tabor's credit he never went whimpering to his son for help. Rather, although past sixty-five, he returned to Leadville to work as a common laborer, wheeling slag to the smelter for $3.00 a day. Run-down in health, with his spirit almost broken, he eventually returned to Baby Doe. By this time her jewels and the children's trinkets were pawned, the former later being sold at a sheriff's sale.

When all seemed lost, Senator Edward Wolcott, once Tabor's political enemy, who had met the beautiful Baby Doe during her Central City days, recommended that Republican President McKinley appoint Tabor postmaster of Denver—in the building standing on that same ground which the former bonanza king had practically given the government "for the erection of the finest post office in the West." In 1898 a grateful old man—for with all his troubles Tabor had grown old—was "stunned at the information" that finally the Republicans had remembered his former generosity. His salary would be $3,500 annually—"Sufficient to rescue him from penury."

Tabor, content to be working again, moved into one room at the Windsor Hotel, where he accepted his reverses without complaining. About one investment he had been right: his second wife. She had not deserted him in his time of trouble, as everybody in Denver predicted. She was still his beautiful Baby Doe.

The year was now 1899; in a few months the twentieth century would begin. Tabor had successfully held his government position as Postmaster of Denver for a year and three months when in April he collapsed with a severe pain in his side. The doctor diagnosed the ailment as appendicitis, calling in two colleagues for consultation. An immediate operation was suggested but Baby Doe, horrified at the thought of surgery, especially for a man of sixty-nine, refused.

Scorning the help of another woman, she nursed him for the seven awful days and nights of his illness. Toward the end his appendix ruptured and peritonitis set in. Just before he sank into a coma she sent for a Roman Catholic priest who baptized Tabor into her church. His last audible words were directed at Baby Doe: "Hang on to the Matchless," he told her. "Someday it will make millions again."

At nine o'clock on the morning of April 10, the doctors informed her that the end was near. Maxcy and Luella were sent for, although the former had not been on friendly terms with his father since the days of the divorce. Tabor did not know them when they arrived and Baby Doe, worn out by her constant vigil, completely broke down. Hysterical, she was led into an adjoining room where shortly afterwards news was brought her that Tabor had died. Half crazed, she refused to believe the truth, insisting that she still had to minister to his needs.

When she had recovered from the first shock she remembered her husband's admonition, "Hang on to the Matchless," and silently vowed never to let it go.

If Denver had not accorded Tabor proper gratitude while he lived, the city fathers more than made up for the omission when he died. A clipping from Baby Doe's own scrapbooks shows her satisfaction that her husband's body lay in state in the Colorado State Capitol and that "the display of blossoms and floral designs about the casket" was "the most elaborate ever seen in this city." Tabor would have appreciated that, she thought, knowing his love of showmanship. Even better would he have liked the belated recognition that, ironically, only his death had brought Baby Doe. She received letters of sympathy from the Governor of Colorado, the state legislature, the Mayor of Denver, Denver City Council and all the civic and fraternal orders. The Tabors' small suite at the hotel was filled with flowers. Lillie and Silver were kept busy receiving the hundreds of telegrams that arrived from far and near. "Papa would be so happy if he could but know," their distracted mother cried.

Every federal, state and city building flew its flag at half mast. Thousands passed by the bier in the

Capitol. Newspaper artists sketched panoramic views of the splendid scene, where at night four soldiers of the State Militia stood guard over the catafalque. Baby Doe's favorite floral tribute was a cornucopia of roses six feet high, sent by the people of Leadville. "He would be most pleased with that gift," she explained to her children. "Your papa really loved Leadville." She also thought but did not tell them that the cornucopia was a symbol of plenty . . . the vanished Tabor plenty.

Ten thousand people lined the streets for a funeral worthy of a Silver King. First ceremonies were in the Capitol, followed by a procession of federal and state soldiers, police and Tabor's beloved firemen, Baby Doe riding in a carriage preceding the glass hearse. Four priests took part in the actual service held in Sacred Heart Church, Denver. During his oration, Father Edward Barry said, "But the whips and scourges of adversity came upon him, and those once his friends turned their backs on him. He did not despair but bared his arms and went to work once more. Here, young men and old, is a lesson in perseverance."

Baby Doe, heavily veiled, was attended by her two children and various relatives. Maxcy and Luella were there, although they acknowledged neither the former's stepmother nor the two little half-sisters. It was an impressive occasion, with the somber, tolling bell, rich organ music, acolytes with swinging censers and sunlight shining through the stained-glass windows.

THE BEGINNING OF THE END

Through the proceedings Baby's sobbing could not be stifled. After the interment at Calvary Cemetery she refused to leave with the other mourners, sitting by the graveside while the earth was thrown in.

At last it was night and she was alone with her dead, for even the gravediggers had gone. It was strange, but sitting there alone with the bright moonlight illuminating the distant Rockies, all she could recall were the words of an old Cheyenne Indian death song:

> *Nothing lives long*
> *Except the earth*
> *And the mountains . . .*

Chapter Ten

The Greek Tragedy

A YEAR after her husband's death Baby Doe wrote, "Nothing received, nothing paid out."

Penned in ink upon ordinary ruled paper and beginning, "In the name of the benevolent Father of all," Tabor's will was worthless, for he had nothing but burdens to leave. The will, drawn up on March 14, 1884, in Leadville, bequeathed everything "to my beloved wife, Elizabeth B. Tabor," asking her to make adequate provision for any heirs. Following his death, among the claims against the estate was an amount of $652.50 for his funeral expenses, including $325 for the casket.

Stratton, the bonanza king who had saved the precious Matchless by advancing Tabor the $15,000 when it was about to be sold to satisfy a court judgment, before Tabor's death had secured the title in Baby Doe's name. He had also generously sent back the unpaid ninety-day note, together with the deed to the Arizona mine which Tabor insisted he should take as security. Stratton had assured Tabor that never had he "contemplated the retention of your note and papers as evidence of indebtedness."

He returned them with his "best wishes and goodwill for your future success." Unfortunately for Baby Doe and her daughters, the Matchless seemed exhausted.

After his death an iron safe, valued at $240 and pawned by Tabor in 1896 for $140, was to figure in one of the several court suits. When she proved that it was her own personal property, it was restored to Baby Doe. After the bank crash Tabor had pawned the family jewels, which included Baby's exotic serpentine girdle and the famed Isabella diamond, which were eventually sold by the sheriff in 1901, although the family had up to Tabor's death paid interest of $2,809.01 upon the original sum received for them.

For two years Baby Doe, Lillie and Silver struggled on in Denver while Baby Doe made endless trips in a vain endeavor to persuade bankers and business men to lend her the money to repossess and improve the Matchless—soon, like everything else, to come up at a sheriff's sale.

Lillie, no doubt remembering the pampered elegance of her youth, lived in a silent, aloof world of her own, scorning her mother's desire to get the Matchless working in order, as Tabor had predicted, to re-establish their lost fortune. Now seventeen years old, the rebellious "Golden Eagle," as Baby Doe called her, bitterly complained, "It's all rot, there being any millions in that hole in the ground. Why, that mine was completely worked out years ago." Such cruel disdain hurt Baby Doe, especially as the younger, twelve-year-old Silver was so warm and loyal to her father's wishes and memory.

In July, 1901, Claudia McCourt bought back the Matchless, saving it this time for Baby Doe. Claudia was the one sister who had remained faithful to her. Now, thought Baby Doe, everything would work out. She would take the girls "home" to Leadville. Silver was thrilled at the prospect of living in the mountain city, but Lillie, having grown utterly alien to her mother's desires, said nothing. Often Baby Doe thought that the wrong Mrs. Tabor had borne her. By coincidence the Tabors took rooms at 303 Harrison Avenue, Leadville—the very house where Jacob Sandelowsky had lived in years gone by.

Lillie hated Leadville, spending most of her time alone in her rooms writing to friends in Denver, but little Silver soon made many new acquaintances, having inherited from Tabor a warmth that drew people to her immediately. Perhaps she was too trusting and friendly, as he had been in the early days, when to Augusta's disapproval he had helped many a stranger. She adored her mother with a sweetness that could only remind the lonely Baby Doe of Tabor's lavish love throughout their married life.

Perhaps Lillie was jealous. In any case, she secretly wrote her uncle Peter McCourt in Denver for help. He responded by sending his niece the fare to reach the McCourt relatives then living in Chicago. Baby Doe could hardly believe her ears when she heard of Lillie's decision to desert her—Lillie, the little Silver Princess who used to dance in the Tabor Box at the Tabor Grand Opera House in Denver—Lillie, upon whom Tabor had lavished so much affection! The last time Baby Doe ever saw her elder daughter was the morning she drove off to the railroad station in a hired buggy. She did not kiss her mother good-bye; neither did she look back. Lillie disappeared out of her mother's life forever, never replying to any of her future communications.

The day that Lillie went away, Baby Doe turned to the church for succor and strength, and often after that visited the Leadville Church of the Annunciation for quiet periods of meditation and prayer. Looking at the imitation frescoes of saints on the wall, she was struck by her own ignorance of their names. One day, upon leaving the church she visited the library and obtained a book entitled *The Lives of the Saints*, which she enjoyed so much that she soon possessed her own

copy. This book and the Bible were her daily companions for the rest of her life. Her favorite saint was
Teresa of Avila, for she liked to read of her grit and
determination in the face of what seemed to be insur-
mountable difficulties, and she found Teresa's mystical
qualities particularly fascinating.

Baby Doe feared the reaction that Lillie's sudden
departure might have upon her younger, more sensitive
sister, but Silver took the news with more indignation
than sorrow. "Good riddance to bad rubbish," she cried,
throwing her arms around her mother's neck. Then,
hand-in-hand and dressed in miners' overalls, Baby Doe
and the child of her great love trudged up the dusty
road to the waiting Matchless on Fryer Hill.

With a burro to haul away ore samples they worked
all that summer at the mine. The hurt in Baby's heart
over Lillie was at times eased when Silver composed
little poems about the wild flowers and distant, waiting mountains. Sentimental Baby Doe kept them all.
Silver even wrote to the fairies and the Man in the
Moon. At Christmas time Santa Claus was mailed a
particularly amusing letter asking not for material gifts
but that they would again find a rich silver lode in
the Matchless.

Even as a little thing Silver was determined that
one day she would grow up to become a famous authoress, bringing honor once more to the Tabor name. All
they had left in the world now was their pride. One
wonders whether, if Augusta had been alive and loving

Tabor as she professed to do, for his sake she might not have helped his child with her literary ambitions. Baby Doe thought it ironic that Augusta, who had always been so fond of journalists and had contributed items to Eastern newspapers, should have possessed the same literary interest as Silver. Perhaps, Baby thought, all the tragic frustrations that had plagued Tabor, Augusta and herself would be righted by Silver. When Lillie departed, Silver had declared, "Don't let her hurt your feelings, Mama. She'll be sorry. When I'm a great authoress and you're a rich society woman in Denver, she'll come running back. Then she'll think differently about the Tabor name."

Silver was already writing poems for her teacher at school. Henry Butler, the kindly editor of the Leadville *Herald-Democrat,* took pity on the child, lending her a typewriter, encouraging her and offering constructive criticism. As she advanced into young womanhood, Silver Dollar's sweet, lisping voice further enhanced her charms. Convent-educated, she had inherited Baby Doe's fine carriage, culture and graciousness. Unfortunately, as she grew older, her courtesy and sensitivity were offset by violent fits of tantrums and anger. Often she entered a romantic world of her own making, and upon leaving it would confuse fiction with truth, but with all her failings she had two great virtues—Tabor's pride and Baby Doe's loyalty.

Sometimes the Matchless was leased to provide small sums sufficient only to house and clothe Baby Doe and

Silver. They rented a tiny house on Seventh Street, and later another at Tenth Street, but never did the earnings procured from the Matchless keep the wolf far from their door.

Although Baby Doe was good at figures she failed hopelessly at managing her mine. The time came when it became necessary to go to Denver, open her safety deposit box and sell the last of her jewels. She was sure, she told Silver, that "dear Tabor would understand." Silver was horrified at even the thought of selling her mother's engagement ring and her father's watch fob—the fob that the people of Denver had given him upon that memorable first night when the Tabor Grand Opera House had opened before an adoring public. The engagement ring comprised a large single pure diamond surrounded by sapphires; Tabor himself had panned the gold for the setting during the early days in California Gulch.

Silver refused to allow her mother to sell the fob. "That must be our talisman," she declared. "We must never part with that." Edgar C. McMechen told Silver that he thought her papa's fob was of great historical interest. In his booklet "The Tabor Story" he writes of "the famous Tabor watch-fob, which Silver once said would never be sacrificed even if it meant that she and her mother must starve."

To save further rent Baby Doe and Silver moved into the one-room cabin up at the mine. "It's just like living on top of the world," Silver cheerfully explained

to a stranger. In the winters they sometimes went to
Denver where Baby Doe, no longer a figure of fashion
as once she had been, continually tried to persuade
somebody to invest in the Matchless. She was sure a
new fortune lay buried there, just as Tabor had said.
Never once did she doubt the truth of her late husband's words.

Two Denver ladies, then teen-age girls, recall vividly
the times that Baby Doe came to their mother's homes
to solicit interest in her beloved Matchless. Mrs. Chloe
Russell remembers being rather disappointed at being
told that the faded, tired-looking woman wearing a
man's large fedora hat (Tabor's, no doubt, for he loved
them) and miner's boots several sizes too big, was the
legendary Baby Doe—the "most beautiful woman in
the West." Yet her youthful disappointment was immediately dispelled when Baby Doe spoke in a "voice
pure as crystal."

Mrs. Laurena Senter recalls,

> When she came to see Mother to ask help in sav-
> ing the Matchless Mine from the mortgagees, she
> seemed anything but glamorous.
>
> The picture that lingers in my memory of her was
> of a woman clothed in dark material, of an outdated
> mode. She wore a visored cap, of the type once used
> as fashionable auto wear. The cap was purple and the
> veil was green. I seem to recall that she wore what
> appeared to be men's shoes.
>
> Pity for her lingered in my mind during all the

years that followed and I was glad when I read that one generous woman ["The Unsinkable Molly Brown"] had made it possible for her to live out her time at her beloved Matchless Mine, which seemed to be an omen of good to her.

In 1910, Silver, then almost twenty-one, gave her mother the greatest happiness she had known since losing Tabor. She had written a lyric entitled "Our President Roosevelt's Colorado Hunt," described as a "March Song," which Professor A.S. Lohmann of Denver set to music. Baby Doe, always ready to make sacrifices where Silver was concerned, saved up for two years for its publication. The cover had rather a startling crimson portrait of the President, which was certainly arresting to the eye, although Baby Doe wished he didn't have to be depicted wearing "those awful pince-nez" spectacles which always reminded her of Augusta. The song was dedicated to "the memory of the late U.S. Senator H.A.W. Tabor." This pleased Baby Doe immensely, for only Silver, who had met the President when he visited Leadville in 1908, would think of surprising her like that. So impressed had Silver been that, returning to the family cabin, she had written the lyric. She also wrote other songs, entitled "Love and Lilies," "Spirits," "The Outlaw Horse," and "In a Dream I Loved You." Unsold copies of her "Colorado Hunt" song, water-marked from storage in one of Baby Doe's leaky trunks, are now collectors' items, although they did the young writer little good at the time of their first appearance.

The chorus ran:

> *Wrapped in a Navajo blanket*
> *In the land of bliss,*
> *Blazing the daring hunter's trail,*
> *Free in the wilderness;*
> *The bugle call of the wild, wild West*
> *Is the Coyote's cry in the hour of rest,*
> *Warm in my Navajo blanket,*
> *I'll live life at its best.*

How proud Baby Doe was of the local notice Silver received for her song! The *Denver Post* even published a two-column picture of her daughter. On August 29, 1910, Roosevelt, then no longer President, visited Denver when a great parade was held, the banners bearing such slogans as "Bully for you, Teddy," and "Deelighted." Teddy was taken to Overland Park for a special Press Club Church Wagon Eat where he ate in true cowboy style. There, with Boy Scouts looking on, Silver was presented to the former President, who expressed great pleasure at the song she had written in his honor. If some people laughed at her efforts, bluff, genuine Teddy Roosevelt, one of the greatest of all American Presidents, did not. He had heard the story of the Tabor tragedy and was deeply touched.

Baby Doe was beside herself with joy as she trudged off to take some wild flowers to the sisters who were

always so good to her at St. Vincent's Hospital, later
pausing for a prayer of gratitude in the church next
door. Had she not entertained a President of the United
States at her wedding? Now a Tabor was again asso-
ciating with Presidents. Surely the old luck would
return.

Unfortunately this was not to be. Instead, Baby Doe
was to experience fresh heartbreak, this time because
of her sole remaining joy, Silver, the "Honeymaid." A
girl with Silver's beauty did not go unnoticed by the
opposite sex. Unknown to her mother she had become
very friendly with the owner of a large white horse—
and Silver loved riding. Matters came to a head at an
Easter Monday ball held in Leadville which Silver attended in a new silk dress made by her mother, and
a fur-trimmed coat. The party was a perfectly respectable one or Baby Doe would never have allowed her
to attend. All Silver's life her mother had overly protected her—or believed that she had. Silver was escorted
by two sons from good Leadville families. All night long
her mother waited, but it was not until eight o'clock
next morning that a completely intoxicated Silver
returned home, coatless, her splendid new dress in
threads.

By the time Silver was herself again, Baby Doe had
made a decision. Silver must go to Denver for her own
good. All Leadville was talking about the escapade of
the night before, to mention nothing of the man with
the horse, of whose relations with Silver Baby Doe had

suspected nothing. Subdued and tearful, Silver wrote her Uncle Peter McCourt, for Baby Doe was too proud herself to write the brother she hated. "Tell him that you want to work on a newspaper but need the fare." Baby Doe had mortgaged the Matchless again and was having trouble with the eight per cent interest payments.

Once more Uncle Peter responded as he had done when Lillie wanted to leave home. Silver left for Denver, "to find," as her mother said, "a man more worthy of her." She worked for a spell as a reporter on the *Denver Times*. To her credit, and unlike Lillie, she sent home a large part of her small weekly salary to help Baby Doe. After a stay in Chicago, she returned to her native Colorado with the observation, "Bright lights, music, revelry have no charm for me. Give me the freedom to do and to dare close to nature as nature bids . . . Chicagoans look sad. They do not know what the buoyancy of right living means."

In spite of her spell of homesickness in the Windy City she had found time to write a novella entitled *Star of Blood,* with a notorious criminal named Allen Hence Downen as the hero. It seemed that subconsciously Silver was drawn towards a less fortunate type of mankind. Lurid and amateurish as her plot may have been, some of the descriptive paragraphs in her story were filled with a strange, sensitive beauty. There was a premonition of tragedy about the book, almost as if it were a prelude to what would happen in Silver's

own life. Once more Baby produced (almost miracu-
lously where her beloved Silver was concerned) the
money to put the manuscript, illustrated with her
daughter's own drawings, between agreeable-looking
mottled gray covers.

Silver's next literary excursion was a little society
gossip paper, *The Silver Dollar Weekly,* which unfortunately folded after the first few issues. Defeated and
lonely, Silver now spent most of her days wandering
from one Denver movie house to another. When she
was twenty-two, one afternoon she was sent by her
mother on an errand to a Denver businessman, who
made advances towards the mentally disturbed girl and
succeeded in seducing her. After this experience Silver
was never the same, but Baby Doe did not realize it
until several years later. Next Silver fell in love with
a man who was more interested in leasing the Matchless from her mother than in marrying the moody,
unpredictable girl. Baby Doe, suspicious that Silver's
beau was plotting to deprive them of their one remaining asset, managed to thwart the romance.

Outraged, Silver quarreled bitterly with the mother
she had always adored and in spite of Baby Doe's tearful pleas, left the Matchless cabin. Her first act was
to declare in writing:

TO WHOM IT MAY CONCERN . . .
I, Silver Tabor, this March 17, 1914, at 2:40 A.M.,
state that I am going insane or something else. If I

[219]

am insane, place me in a Catholic institution . . . My
head is covered with self-inflicted bruises and my
heart is weak and my lungs congested, for I am a
frail girl, a nervous wreck from the life I live. The
only chance I have is to be separated from her [Baby
Doe], *as I try to kill myself all the time . . .*

Night after night, Silver went the rounds of Leadville, visiting friends, drinking, living in second-rate
boarding houses and hotels. Night after night, the
frantic Baby Doe trailed her psychopathic daughter.
Once she appeared at one of Silver's parties, scattering
her dubious friends with a few well-chosen Irish epi-
thets. Furious, the next day Silver sent her mother a
letter saying, "under no circumstances will I have anything more to do with you." However as soon as Silver's
finances ran out she wrote her mother again, begging
for help, and accusing her of ruining her life by not
leasing the Matchless to the man who "wanted to marry
me." Baby Doe often descended hundreds of feet into
the mine to scratch out a miserable amount of ore to
sell, in order to satisfy her temperamental Silver's needs.
She was haunted by fears of what would happen to
her precious "Honeymaid," fears that were increased
by a terrible dream she had experienced on the night
of Wednesday, May 7, 1913. Carefully next morning
she had noted it down:

I dreamed Silver sat in a rocking chair and her
hands were up to her face and were very red and

*she was crying and telling me, "Oh, mama, I'm crazy.
I have gone mad!" And her heart was broken and I
was heartbroken at her grief.*

Silver never left her mother in peace for long, for
there was always some personal crisis at hand. On one
occasion, although only living in a rooming house, she
bought a piano on the hire-purchase system; but of
course, being Silver, she soon ran out of money and
was unable to keep up the payments. A frantic note
was dispatched up to the Matchless, which as usual
met with a satisfactory response.

"My Darling Silver," wrote Baby Doe, "I send you
with this $10. Don't let anyone take your piano. I will
fix it all O.K. Your loving Mama." Baby Doe might
just as well have kept her ten dollars, for in no time
Silver's ambitions to be a great pianist had vanished
into thin air.

Abortive careers as a movie actress, a waitress and
a chorine ended when a drunken dancer mistakenly
accused Silver of stealing a ring. Although the accuser
found the piece of jewelry in her own possession the
next day, the situation left a lasting stigma on Silver's
disturbed mind. She left Colorado, never to return, and
on tour as an Egyptian belly dancer she was stranded
penniless and pregnant in Nebraska when the show
folded. A miscarriage followed, complicated by peritonitis and blood poisoning.

In despair after the collapse of another love affair,
Silver resolved to enter a convent, but over the next

few years her mother received letters from various cheap boarding houses under different names. A chronic alcoholic and drug addict, Silver died in agony in an apartment on Chicago's seamy Ellis Avenue, evidently from burns and shock suffered when, drying her hair by a radiator, she upset a pan of boiling water. Horrified neighbors, summoned by her screams, found her naked and glassy-eyed, writhing in torture, in an apartment with five terrified cats.

In her novella *Star of Blood* Silver had written her own epitaph:

> *It was all ended . . . No more would she rove the streets bareheaded, with the winter wind pitilessly cutting her half-naked body, in a mad effort to find food and shelter; never again would she be found drunk in the Market street gutters . . .*

It was September 18, 1925. Back in Colorado, Baby Doe was visiting Denver. As she returned to her cheap hotel one night the clerk, full of curiosity, blurted out, "Is that your daughter who I see in the paper tonight was murdered in some Chicago scandal?"

The blood in Baby Doe's veins turned to ice; then, recovering her composure, she managed to say, "Certainly not. My daughter is in a convent." Without another word she hurried off to reach the Denver Public Library before the newspaper files closed at half-past nine, for she could not spare even the few cents needed to buy her own paper. The kindly librarian, realizing the identity of the black-clad, wraithlike figure with the faded old motoring cap and heavy boots, guessed her tragic errand. Making an exception, she brought the once lovely Mrs. Tabor the *Denver Post*. Baby Doe clutched the reading table as the headlines screamed, SILVER DOLLAR SLAIN BY FIENDS OF CHICAGO SLUMS.

Grimly she read every word, then carefully folded the newspaper and handed it back to the surprised librarian.

"Thank you very much for the paper," she said, her voice quite calm, "but that story's all a pack of lies. She's not my daughter—that young woman. I know Silver is in a convent."

For the rest of her life Baby Doe never admitted to the world that the thirty-six-year old woman who had died in such horrible circumstances in a disreputable section of Chicago's third ward was in reality her favorite daughter. However, when Baby Doe left the Public Library on that fateful night she managed to get together the cost of sending Lillie a telegram to say that Silver was dead. She did not receive a reply, although *The Chicago Tribune*, on September 21, 1925, printed a statement from Lillie which said,

> *"I never approved of her; she looked at life so differently. I can see no more reason now why she should be more to me than just a dead woman down in Chicago. Why should I, who have pride and position, and like only quiet and nice things, have to claim her now in this kind of death."*

In the end, to save her from a pauper's grave, the neighbors on Ellis Street collected funds for Silver Dollar's funeral. One of the McCourt aunts went to the morgue to identify the body. Sure that it was her own flesh and blood, she immediately got in touch with Peter McCourt, who wired $300 for the burial in Holy Sepulchre Cemetery, Chicago. Once more Baby Doe's brother had "helped" the family, although she did not see it that way. In her opinion, by acknowledging the dead woman in Chicago to be his niece he had only brought further humiliation upon her dear Tabor's name.

Alone at the Matchless, Baby Doe carefully recorded her latest dream:

> *Only the angels know her joy and they whisper in the waves and I thank them for releasing her from the world and me. She was born only for the better world and not for man's false heart, but she is my golden lily and with her I cannot part . . . last night . . . thinking I was alone I cried to the wind and waves to bring her back . . . bring her back . . .*

Chapter Eleven

Eventide

So Baby Doe grew old. Sustained always by the memory of the great love of her "dear Tabor" and fortified with deep religious faith, she watched the seasons come and go. Best of all she loved April, heralding the coming of spring. Then the icy snow melted around her lonely cabin and myriads of wild flowers burst into fragrant blossom. August was the month of the goldenrod. Soon she knew the aspens turned to gold; winter with its lonely hours would not be far away.

Dressed in a long black skirt and ancient coat, her

legs bundled up with burlap and twine, she occasionally walked into Leadville to fetch her few provisions
from the ever-understanding Zaitz grocery store. In the
icy winter months she pinned newspapers under her
ragged clothing to stimulate warmth in her thin body.
She was never without her ancient motoring cap with
veil and visor—the same that young Laurena Senter
had noticed when Baby Doe had visited her mother so
many years before. Now the purple cap and its once-
fashionable green veil were a dirty faded gray. Not a
wisp of hair was allowed to show; like a nun's, it was
severely hidden from the world. Always at her breast
was pinned a crucifix while in her hand she carried a
mysterious black leather handbag. Creeping into town
like a wraith from another world . . . It was incredible
that this was the woman whose appearance at the
Tabor Grand Opera House, Denver, on an April evening in 1883 had distracted the audience from the great
tragedian Lawrence Barrett. Baby Doe told Father
Horgan a few months before she died, "I had all the
enjoyment I wanted when I was young. I do not need
enjoyment now!"

Often during the winter, when Mrs. Tabor arrived
in town too late for the grocery boys to help her home
before dark with her purchases, she would stay overnight at the home of Mrs. Mary Mandl. It was the
logical place to stay, Mrs. Mandl insisted, being located
in the Keystone Block where Tabor once had a suite.
Baby Doe rather disrupted the household, Mrs.

Mandl's daughter recalls, because she would say her prayers aloud and keep them awake.

Still wearing her faded motoring cap, Baby Doe would sit in a chair staring out of the window at the snow-covered mountains. One day young Theresa plucked up her courage and asked, "Why do you cover up all your pretty hair?"

"Well, my dear," Baby Doe answered with a knowing smile, "when one is a penitent, one must hide one's beauty."

Late in 1932, Denver was the scene of the première of the screen adaptation of *Silver Dollar*, David Karsner's book dealing with the Tabors. The author was coming all the way from New York to address the gala audience, while distinguished Leadville citizens were traveling to Denver by special train. The crowning touch to the great occasion would be the actual presence of Baby Doe Tabor to witness the screening of her own life story, but Mrs. Tabor refused. Even the Mayor of Leadville could not budge her from the windblown cabin on Fryer Hill.

Offers of money—even the securing of the mortgage on the Matchless—could not induce her to go. However, she did give them a little of the Matchless ore to be displayed in the theatre foyer.

Writers speculate freely on her devotion to the old mine. Caroline Bancroft says, ". . . perhaps after she had fruitlessly worked the abandoned drifts she came to realize that the Matchless was truly gutted, that

geologically the rich ore had lain in a pocket formation
which had been emptied and that Tabor, who was no
miner, had been wrong. In that event, her lonely thirty-
five year vigil was a dedication to the man she loved
and expiation for past sins. The Matchless was an altar
where, with her life as a lighted candle, she held per-
petual service—and upon which she finally sacrificed
herself."

"The world may have regarded Mrs. Tabor as a little
queer," said Frank Zaitz, proprietor of the Zaitz Mercantile Store, in a press interview given at the time of
her death, "but we, who knew her, knew that was not
true. She was a fine, friendly woman. Until the last
she was shrewd too, in her business way, and was
capable of drawing up a legal contract which would
do credit to a lawyer."

Checking through Baby Doe's final scrapbook made
from a cheap, coverless ledger, now bound together
with linen backing, one can verify the truth of Mr.
Zaitz's statement, for even though nearing eighty, she
was excellent at figures. Each purchase is recorded
down to the last cent.

Other reliable people have left valuable eye-witness
records of Baby Doe during these closing years, which
tend to contradict the rumors of her senility.

The Western History Department of the Denver Public Library possesses an interesting firsthand description of Mrs. Tabor, written during this latter period of
her life and attributed to that same Henry C. Butler,

EVENTIDE

Editor of the *Leadville-Democrat* who had been so kind to Silver Dollar when she was striving to become a writer:

"Oh, I cannot accept charity," she says, "I believe that I would rather starve. Yes, I would rather die." Foolish pride, some say; but to know the Tabor pride is to realize that hunger and cold are nothing beside the suffering it would have to undergo. . . . Packages left on her doorstep are invariably returned to their donors, unopened. With amazing shrewdness the old lady determines who has brought them and back they go. Once when she was unable to trace a box of cast-off clothing, she stopped in at the local newspaper office and requested a notice be run asking the persons responsible to call for their offering. On the box she wrote: "Such an insult. I hope never again." . . .

Mrs. Tabor is a little bewildered at the return of the Tabor name to fame in recent years. But she has become more or less accustomed, during tourist season, to the stream of curious people who climb the winding road to her humble cabin. By the hundreds they come, to get a look at this queer old recluse, expecting to see her step out of the pages of a book, no doubt. Only a few even catch a glimpse of her—she stays close within her retreat. But she keeps a watchful eye at one of the little windows when a stranger ventures too close to the mine. She trusts no one; in every unknown visitor she sees a schemer who would get the Matchless away from her. Rumors have long persisted that she keeps a shotgun handy and would not hesitate to use it if her suspicions were aroused.

On the door of her rude cabin generally appears a note: "See watchman at side door." The watchman, like the nonexistent side door, cannot be found. Once there was a George Schmitt, a dwarfed and eccentric old miner who helped Mrs. Tabor "guard" the mine. He lived in a little shack by the old shaft house. An extremely cold spell came late in the spring of 1930 and one morning, when he did not appear as usual, Mrs. Tabor went to his little place. His stiffened body was in a chair beside his little stove. The fire had died out and the poor old fellow had been too chilled either to move to rebuild it or cry out for help.

Since then, Mrs. Tabor has been quite alone.

On a Sunday afternoon I sometimes go up Fryer hill for a visit with the queer old lady. Always it is a toss-up whether or not she will remember me—if she does I am heartily welcomed.

"Come in, come in," she greets me and with a trace of the once grand Tabor manner ushers me in through the lean-to. She offers me a chair in the single barren room that is her home and she sits opposite me. Her thin hands are restless, always twisting a handkerchief or plucking at the tattered dress about her knees. But the sad, faded eyes are always watching me.

For a while she questions me about what is going on, in the town and generally. She asks about silver— is the price going up? For one who so seldom sees a newspaper she seems surprisingly well versed in affairs at large. She has even heard of the latest scandal in the village and asks for the latest developments.

I look about the frail cabin and wonder how it

can ever withstand the wintry blasts that sweep down over the hill from the north.

"Aren't the winters terribly hard on you?" I ask.

"Oh, but no," she replies. "I have such good health. I am quite comfortable. This is just the life for me— God has given me the strength to live here." It seems to me that she may have taken on some of the ruggedness of the surrounding hills. And too, she is very religious, I perceive. On the rough walls are pictures clipped from newspapers depicting the Crucifixion, the Sisters at their kindly work, and on one wall a little wax Virgin in its shrine. My gaze wanders to some cardboard and wooden boxes piled in a corner.

"That is my wardrobe—where I keep my good clothes." As I look back at her, I catch the fleeting smile in her tired eyes.

Then she tells me of the finery that once was hers. She likes to talk of the old days when Tabor was at the height of his fame and the Matchless pouring forth its $2,000 a day. The years seem to fall away from the faded old face. Now she plucks almost daintily at the shabby skirt and I see in the motion the gracefulness of a fine lady gathering her velvet gown about her. I wonder how it can be possible for one who once had so much, to now have so little and yet want to live. Then I realize that she lives not in the same world as I, but in a world of her own creation—a world carried over from the past, peopled with the memories of those who have passed on. And in this world is one magnificent figure—Tabor.

There has been some talk, from time to time, of a monument to Tabor. But I know of a living memorial that could never be approached by carving in cold stone, no matter how great. In the heart and soul of this solitary old woman is the grand remembrance . . . and the Tabor Pride.

At St. Vincent's Hospital, Leadville, the sisters were always kind to the old lady. It was they who helped Baby Doe make the "gun" with which she scared off intruders to her beloved mine. Part of a broom handle was used, the sisters coloring it with burnt cork. The only real gun that Baby Doe ever possessed was given her by a friend and was so old and broken that it wouldn't work anyhow. Later she hocked it for five dollars to buy food.

The Matchless scrapbooks that occupied Baby Doe's later years were not so neat as the large ones she had made as a young woman in Central City, Leadville and Denver. Often it seemed she was badly in need of a pair of scissors, for the newspaper clippings were sometimes torn out and pasted in without trimming. This did nothing, however, to detract from their varied flavor. Baby Doe still knew the secret of making a scrapbook interesting. As usual, she had pressed sprays of wild flowers between the pages—yellow mustard, wild aster and Indian paintbrush. On the back of a Western Union form she scribbled, "Drove me to P.O. about 4 p.m. Lovely folk," and stuck it into her book of memories.

Over a picture of three nuns she sadly wrote, "O if only my poor children could have lived such simple and holy lives. O may God protect them. I am heart-broken and O how I suffer."

Beside the report of a Denver society wedding she commented wryly, "O why couldn't my girls have made marriages like this?"

There were clippings entitled CASTOR OIL AS A FLY POISON, GARLIC REDUCES BLOOD PRESSURE and DRUG ADDICT TURNS AMUSED TITTERS TO SOBS AND CHEERS. HE GAINS HIS FREEDOM. BEAUTIFUL VOICE ENTHRALLS COURT. A visiting card from the old days bears the name, FATHER GUIDA, S.J., SACRED HEART CHURCH.

On another page one finds a poem by Walter Scott Bogart entitled "Juno (An Ode to Womanhood)," with the appropriate lines,

> *She walks alone*
> *The ambient air*
> *Breathes forth the fragrance*
> *Of her Soul.*

Rather pathetic is the piece headed OUR YESTERDAYS:

> *Leadville Forty-Six Years Ago.*
> *Forty-six years ago today, Feb. 11, 1882. From the files of Leadville newspapers:*
> The Herald's *mining column states that Governor Tabor has accepted the presidency of the "great Michoagan syndicate of mines in Old Mexico . . ."*

. . . Mines that were worthless, she would remember. . . .

She even cut out the notice of the death of her stepson, Maxcy Tabor, in 1929: "DEATH OF MAXCY TABOR WRITES NEW LINE IN GRIM TRAGEDY OF PIONEER FAMILY OF COLORADO. . . . Tabor divorced the wife who had toiled by his side and married 'Baby Doe' Tabor, said to have been the most beautiful woman in the West . . . Mrs. Tabor, now living here in poverty, had no relations with her husband's son."

Ironic was the letter—carefully preserved along with others sent right to the end of her life by admirers, detractors and fortune hunters—that was meant for Augusta (then long dead), which instead was delivered to Baby Doe. In part it read, ". . . I used to work for Mrs. Tabor No. 2, and what a woman, a regular roustabout. She tried her best to get in society, but failed."

If Baby Doe did not like a person she could be very outspoken about it, as indicated by the tart remark under the long article on Adelina Patti (1843-1919), one of the great opera singers of her time. Baby Doe commented, "She was rotten, stingy and selfish." Doubtless, as a theater owner's wife, she had found out how temperamental some stars could be.

To the last, Baby Doe made her trips into Leadville to buy groceries. Sometimes the arduous journey in winter time was almost too much for her aging body. After one such trying experience on March 6, 1934, she scribbled across one of her countless calendars:

*Went down to Leadville from Matchless—the snow
so terrible I had to go down on my hands and knees
and creep from my cabin door to 7th Street. Mr. Zait's
driver* [Zaitz delivery truck] *drove me to our get-off
place and he helped pull me up to the cabin. I kept
falling deep down through the snow every minute.
God bless him.*

Yet still Baby Doe struggled on. Rain, snow, tem-
peratures falling to twenty below, rotting timber shafts
and mountain rats—nothing could stop that gallant
spirit. On February 20, 1935, the last day anyone saw
her alive, she managed to walk the mile or so into
Leadville. It was a merciless day, and by the time she
arrived at her destination the gunny sack wrappings
on her feet were soaked with water. Time and again
she had fallen through melting snow crusts into the
slush and streamlets underneath.

Upon reaching the Zaitz Mercantile Store she complained of having a toothache and neuralgia. It was
commented upon at the time, for no one could remember Baby Doe's ever before showing any signs of sick-
ness. Elmer Kutzlub, the delivery boy, drove her home
by truck, letting her off at Little Stray Horse Gulch
just past an old railroad trestle which is now no more.
Clutching her precious bag of groceries, Baby Doe
waved him a grateful good-bye as she struggled up the
steep hillside. The youth did not realize that he was
witnessing the final curtain of the fabulous Tabor Story.

Robert Hopkin had painted a verse from "Old and

New: A Parable" by Charles Kingsley, upon the curtain at the Tabor Grand Opera House, Denver:

> *So fleet the works of men:*
> *Back to the earth again.*
> *Ancient and holy things*
> *Fade like a dream.*

For the next two weeks nothing was seen of Baby Doe, although a friendly neighbor, Sue Bonnie ("Songbird"), did notice smoke coming out of the chimney pipe for part of that time. Then after a bad storm she missed the smoke. On March 7 she tried unsuccessfully to break her way through deep snow drifts to visit her elderly friend. By this time frantic because Baby Doe had prophesied "You'll be the one to find me, when I'm dead," she managed, with the help of Tom French, to reach the isolated cabin.

All was silence and peace. They broke a window to enter. Lying on the floor was the body of Baby Doe Tabor, Silver Queen of Colorado, frozen in the shape of a cross.

EPILOGUE

Epilogue

GOOD AND FAITHFUL BABY DOE—HER VIGIL ENDED.
Once more the Belle of Oshkosh was front page news.
THE QUEEN IS DEAD . . . ANGELS AND DEVILS VISITED
MRS. TABOR DURING LONELY VIGIL . . . PRIDE NEVER DIED.
. . . BABY DOE REACHES THE END OF THE RAINBOW,
Screamed the headlines, yet unlike those of half a century before, these were kind.

Willard McCourt, Baby Doe's brother, arrived in Leadville to make arrangements for her funeral. Reporters approached the woman living in Milwaukee, thought to be Lillie, Baby Doe's missing daughter, but she denied all relationship, declaring herself to be the daughter of another Tabor who in fact never had a daughter. Then a sympathetic public from all parts of the country took a practical part in paying for Baby Doe's funeral. Reading in the newspapers the story of her long tragic vigil, they cabled and mailed their offerings. The heirs of J.K. Mullen, millionaire miller who had paid off the Matchless mortgage for Baby Doe, were extremely generous. The plan to bury her in a grave blasted by dynamite from the frozen earth in St. Joseph's Cemetery, Leadville, was abandoned. Baby Doe would be returned to the scene of her triumphs in Denver.

Baby Doe's frail body had hardly been removed from her meagre cabin when vandals, skeptical that the fabulous Tabor fortune could have evaporated so completely, smashed down the door. They cut and ripped her ancient mattress to pieces in search for a nonexistent fortune, stripped off the layers of wall lining that Baby Doe had laboriously tacked up to keep out the wintry blasts, then scattered her precious scrapbooks and personal papers all over the floor. One more enterprising than the others, disappointed at not finding a fortune, stole her little stove and chimney pipe. Teen-agers, encouraged no doubt by the example of their elders, even took her calendars. By the following August the cabin was a shambles, its windows broken and the battered door hanging by one hinge. The rain poured in.

EPILOGUE

It seems almost prophetic that Baby Doe in her book of personal dreams and visions had written on December 9, 1922, "I saw my private little papers all scattered about . . . When I got up I found I had not bolted my door. I had only locked it with a common key. God watched me and all my papers."

After the vandals had departed with their pickings, historian Caroline Bancroft rescued the faded papers which now form an important part of the interesting Tabor family memorabilia in the Denver Public Library's Western History Department.

On March 13 the inhabitants of the Cloud City gathered in the imposing red brick Church of the Annunciation with its tall slender spire. There Baby Doe's trusted friend, the Reverend Father Edward L. Horgan, conducted a Solemn Requiem Mass, while from above the statues of a benevolent Virgin, St. Anthony and her beloved angels looked kindly down. Baby Doe, with her sense of pageantry, would have liked it.

The night before, holding a small silver crucifix, she had lain in state at the mortuary. The plan that some publicity-seekers had formed to have her buried in a solid silver coffin was fortunately thwarted. A *Rocky Mountain News* editorial said, "There is a talk of a public subscription to purchase a silver casket for Baby Doe. What a sham! Such a gesture would be a mockery of her courage and desires. Should she be given in death that which she would not accept in life?"

In death she wore a neat brown crêpe dress and

new slippers, the latter found still unpacked in a box at her cabin. The most amazing thing about her appearance was the mass of red-flecked golden hair carefully arranged like a young girl's about her shoulders. Luxuriant as in her heyday, it still retained the original color, with hardly a gray hair. Baby Doe had spoken the truth when she told Theresa O'Brien, "When one is a penitent, one must hide one's beauty."

In the *Denver Catholic Register* for June 18, 1953, appeared the following testimony:

> *Baby Doe Tabor, despite the fact that she committed many sins as a younger woman, spent the last part of her life as a true and devoted Catholic. She retired to a life of penance and self-mortification at the Matchless Mine cabin in Leadville. Her best friend and confidant during the final period was Father Horgan of the Church of the Annunciation. She was buried from his church after her body was found frozen in 1935.*

Later, Baby Doe's body was taken to Denver where it was buried in Mount Olivet Cemetery. Horace Tabor was exhumed from his grave in old, abandoned Calvary Cemetery and laid beside her. At long last they were reunited. As their ill-fated daughter Silver had written in her novelette, *Star of Blood*, "Only the grave brings peace."

Augusta lies at Riverside, Denver's pioneer cemetery, in a grave as lonely as the fifteen unhappy years following her divorce from Tabor. In spite of the fact that at death her carefully invested divorce settlement had grown into a million and a half dollars, the last resting place of Augusta Tabor, once known as "The First Lady of Leadville," is marked only by a simple, twelve-dollar, gray granite marker with the brief inscription,

TABOR
AUGUSTA L.
1835 - 1895

There is no curb; only a few white tobacco flowers grow around the grave. In death the first Mrs. Tabor asks nothing of God or man.

POSTSCRIPT

POSTSCRIPT

Postscript

IN 1955, a granite stone honoring Augusta Tabor was erected in the yard of Tabor School, Tabor Valley, south of Manhattan, Kansas. Augusta, whose Denver parties the young folks loved to attend, would surely have approved this form of memorial.

The meager remains of the once-fabulous Tabor estate were later found in St. Vincent's Hospital, Leadville, and at a Denver warehouse. Baby Doe's battered, old-fashioned round top trunks, gunnysacks, cardboard boxes and brown-paper packages contained many a tragic and sentimental reminder of her fleeting years of happiness as Colorado's Silver Queen. Conspicuous was the white moire bridal gown that she had worn at her Washington wedding. The expensive marabou trimming was missing—sold, no doubt, to meet an emergency—as was the body of the prized ermine opera coat of which only the collar and cuffs were left.

Among the clothing were nearly fifty hats, many of them ruined by water when fire attacked the warehouse in which they were stored. There were other dresses belonging to Baby Doe, pathetic baby garments, Tabor's brilliant suspenders, pajamas, wedding vest and especially molded and initialed shaving mug. An engraved gold sword presented to Tabor when he was a general in the Colorado National Guard, a gilded ostrich egg, Baby Doe's dainty nightgowns, three dried ears of corn, a box of the special brand of Tabor cigars, her beautiful ivory toilet set with eye shade to match, a Tiffany tea set, baby Lillie's seed pearl necklace, relics of the Opera House, crumpled letters, Silver Dollar's rejected novels and stories—all came to light with thirty-year-old jars of preserves, empty coffee cans and gunny sacks filled with carefully rolled newspapers bearing outside the instructions, "For Shelving."

However, there seemed to be missing the most important item: the jewel box containing the unique watch-fob presented to H.A.W. Tabor by the citizens of Denver, which Silver Dollar had passionately declared would never be sold "even if Mother and I must starve." The box of purple velvet and gold set with

Colorado gem-stones was found at last in the Denver warehouse—but it was empty.

Some time later when the trunks were opened at St. Vincent's Hospital, Leadville, the watch-fob was found among a bundle of rags, braided into a tightly-bound ball. Edgar C. McMechen comments, "In the center was the fob, symbolic of the manner in which Baby Doe, after Tabor's death, had withdrawn from the world and hidden her grief within a protective shell of silence and reserve."

A group of civic-minded Denver and Colorado Springs residents calling themselves the Tabor Association later acquired the bulk of the trunks' contents at public auction, presenting them to the Colorado State Museum where today they are a great tourist attraction.

In Denver the Tabor name survives in some ways. There is a Denver telephone exchange called TABOR, a superior MATCHLESS restaurant, a delightfully arranged TABOR COLLECTION at the Colorado State Museum and Baby Doe's early scrapbooks in the library of the State Historical Society of Colorado.

The Western History Department at the Public Library, Denver, has a well-documented Tabor collection of news clippings, magazine articles, and books including Augusta Tabor's sad little scrapbooks.

The Tabor Grand Opera House opened with such pomp in September, 1881, is still entertaining the public, but not in the way it was originally intended, for it is now a movie house catering to Spanish-speaking audiences. Although still advertised as "The Pioneer Theater of the West," it has been renamed the Tabor Latin Theater.

Central City, where Baby Doe set up housekeeping with her first husband, Harvey Doe, is currently a tourist Mecca; but it was in Leadville, the Cloud City, where Oscar Wilde is purported to have seen the sign that read

> *Please do not shoot the pianist.*
> *He is doing his best.*

that one still feels the spirit of Baby Doe.

Set ten thousand feet up in the mountains, Leadville itself is a strange mingling of the past and present. Here in the eighteen eighties, Tabor's Matchless Mine produced silver worth $80,000 a month, even being known to hit the $100,000 mark. The people living to-day in what was once known as "Lusty Leadville" are polite and friendly. The dance halls and honky-tonks are gone and their painted ladies with them. On November 30, 1951, the row of old frame cribs on State Street was destroyed by fire. The better things of Leadville seem to have remained.

The Tabor Grand, renamed the Vendome Hotel, is still doing business. In its Cloudy City Restaurant a truly delicious MATCHLESS FILET MIGNON is served.

Outside, streamers strung across the street proclaim

POSTSCRIPT

WELCOME TO LEADVILLE
ALL AMERICAN CITY
MATCHLESS MINE

Augusta's little reddish-brown clapboard house with the gables, now standing on Harrison Avenue, contains a small Tabor Museum. The Tabor Opera House, in which Wilde lectured, and the Church of the Annunciation, scene of Baby Doe's Solemn Requiem Mass, are kept in careful repair.

Outside the Opera House stands a replica of Augusta's first little log-built store, with a sign that announces:

SPECIALS THIS WEEK
BEANS BACON FLOUR COFFEE
LAMPS COAL-OIL TUBS
LANTERNS WASHBOARDS

The Opera House's red announcement board reads, MELODRAMA TICKETS SOLD HERE, and set in the floor are silver numerals to denote the seating, for in the eighties ushers had no flashlights. The plush curtains and boxes are gone but it is still possible to see the spot where Williams Jennings Bryan sat. On stage the floorboards are pegged together with wood, for nails cost a dollar a pound when brought from the East. Tabor's Opera House is a place of ghosts.

The cabin on Fryer Hill with its untidy dumps of ore

specimens spewed from the bowels of the earth itself has been carefully restored as a summer museum, where five carloads of tourists arrive in an equal number of minutes to see where faithful Baby Doe died still guarding the Matchless. Inside, the guide book bears the names of visitors who, having seen the opera *The Ballad of Baby Doe,* have been drawn there from all parts of the world.

There to be seen are the original iron bedstead painted a pinkish-white with brass trimmings; Baby Doe's two worn wicker rockers; an old chest with a broken gray marble top, and even a vase painstakingly covered with Tabor's cigar wrappers. Baby's large handbag, without which she never went anywhere, is carefully preserved. For years the curious conjectured as to what it contained. After her death the bag was found filled only with her cherished newspapers. The design tooled in the leather includes a spray of passion flowers.

Outside, in summer, the wild flowers that Baby Doe loved bloom in profusion: great clumps of vivid yellow mustard, flaming fireweed, pale blue columbines and the palest yellow roses. There is the shaft with the bucket on which four men, standing on the rim and clutching the cable, used to descend into the mine. Close by, a ladder leads down into the blackness where now only the scampering of mountain rats breaks the dead silence.